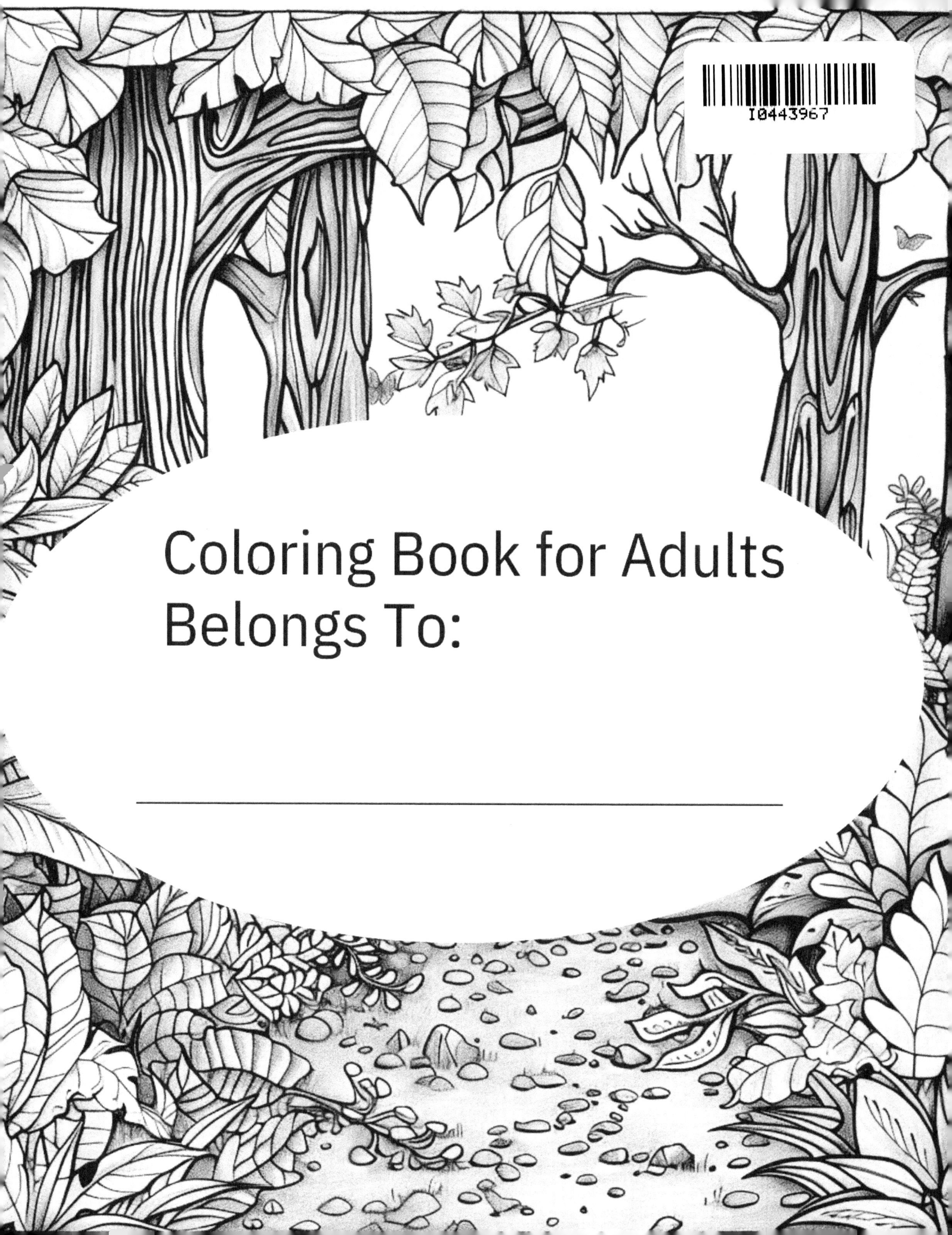

Coloring Book for Adults Belongs To:

____

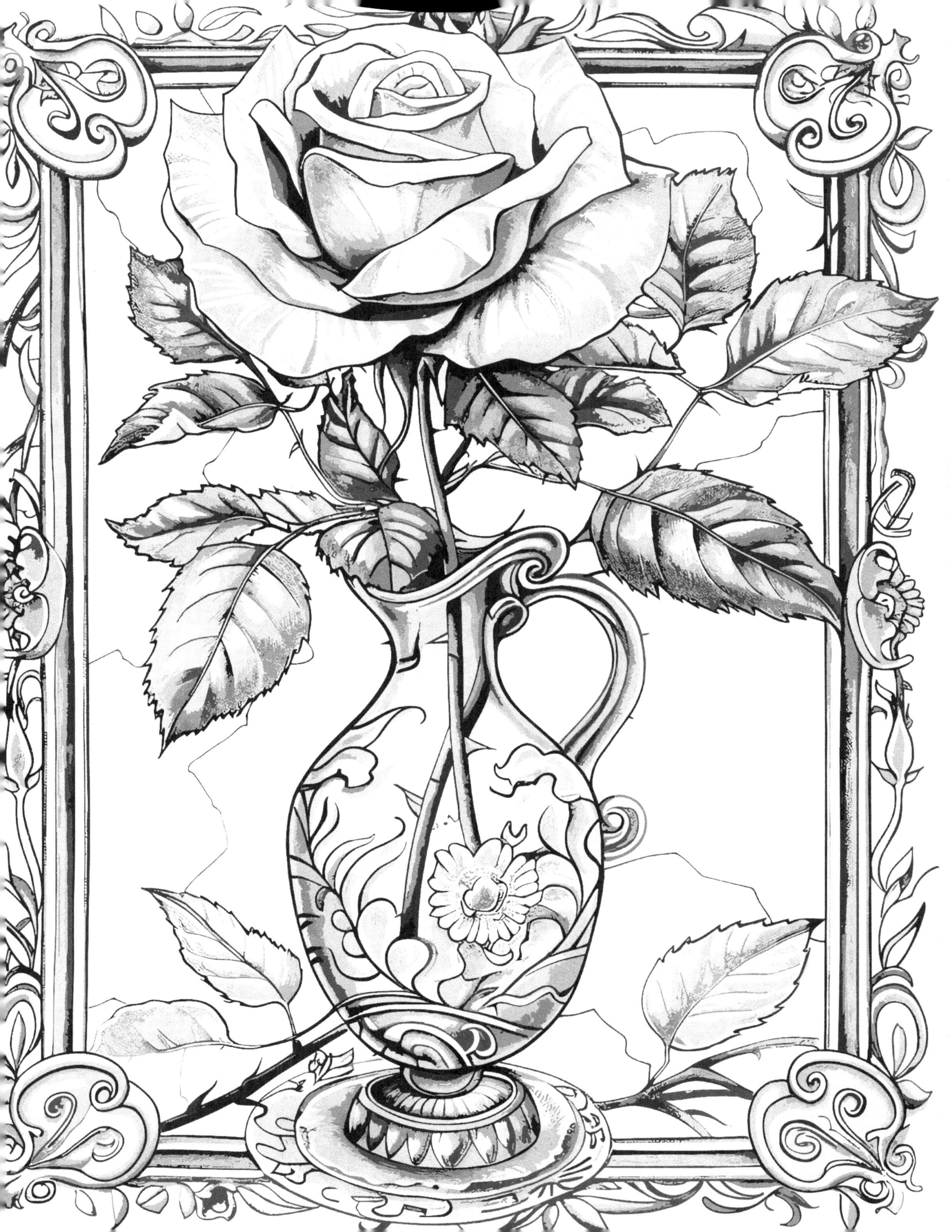

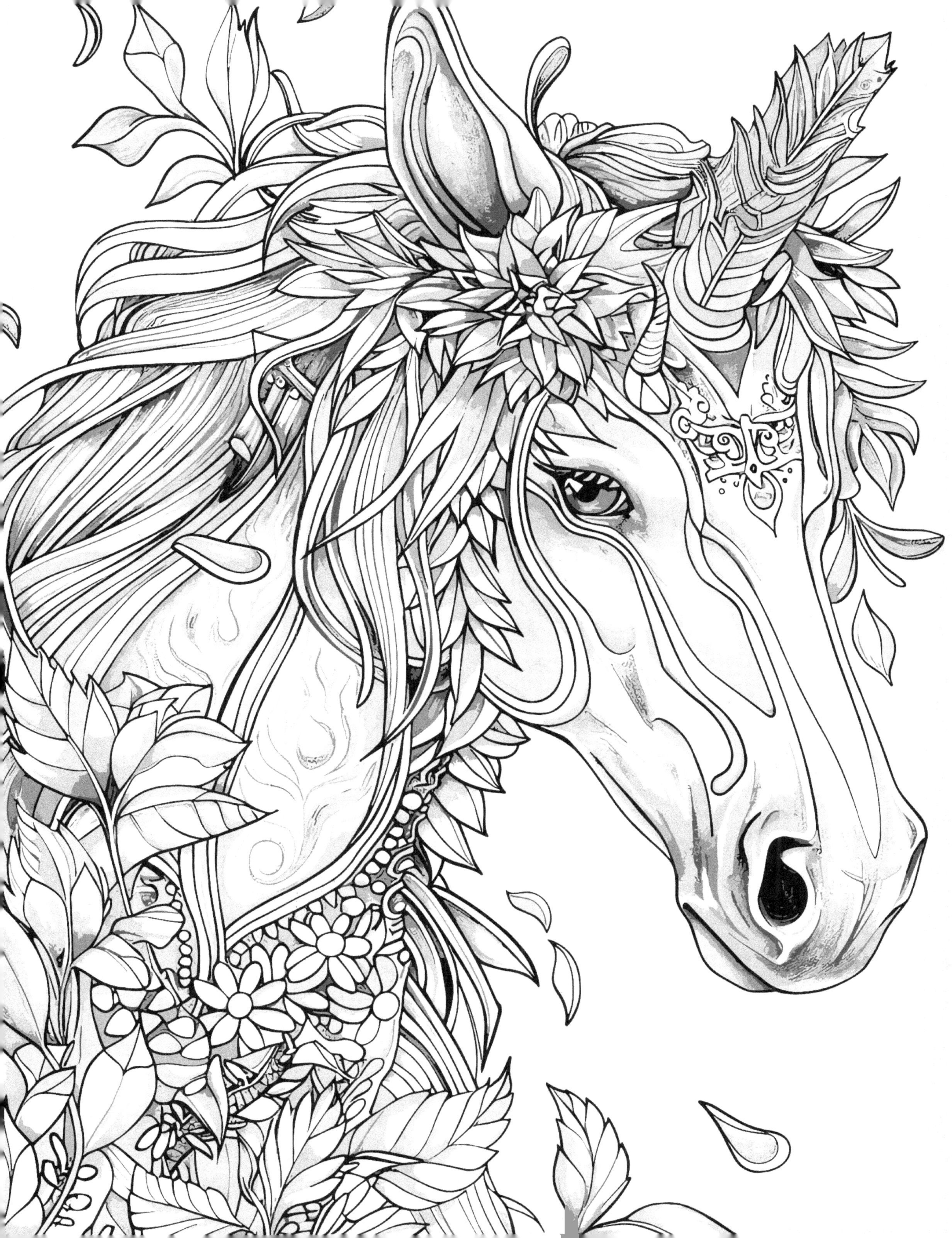

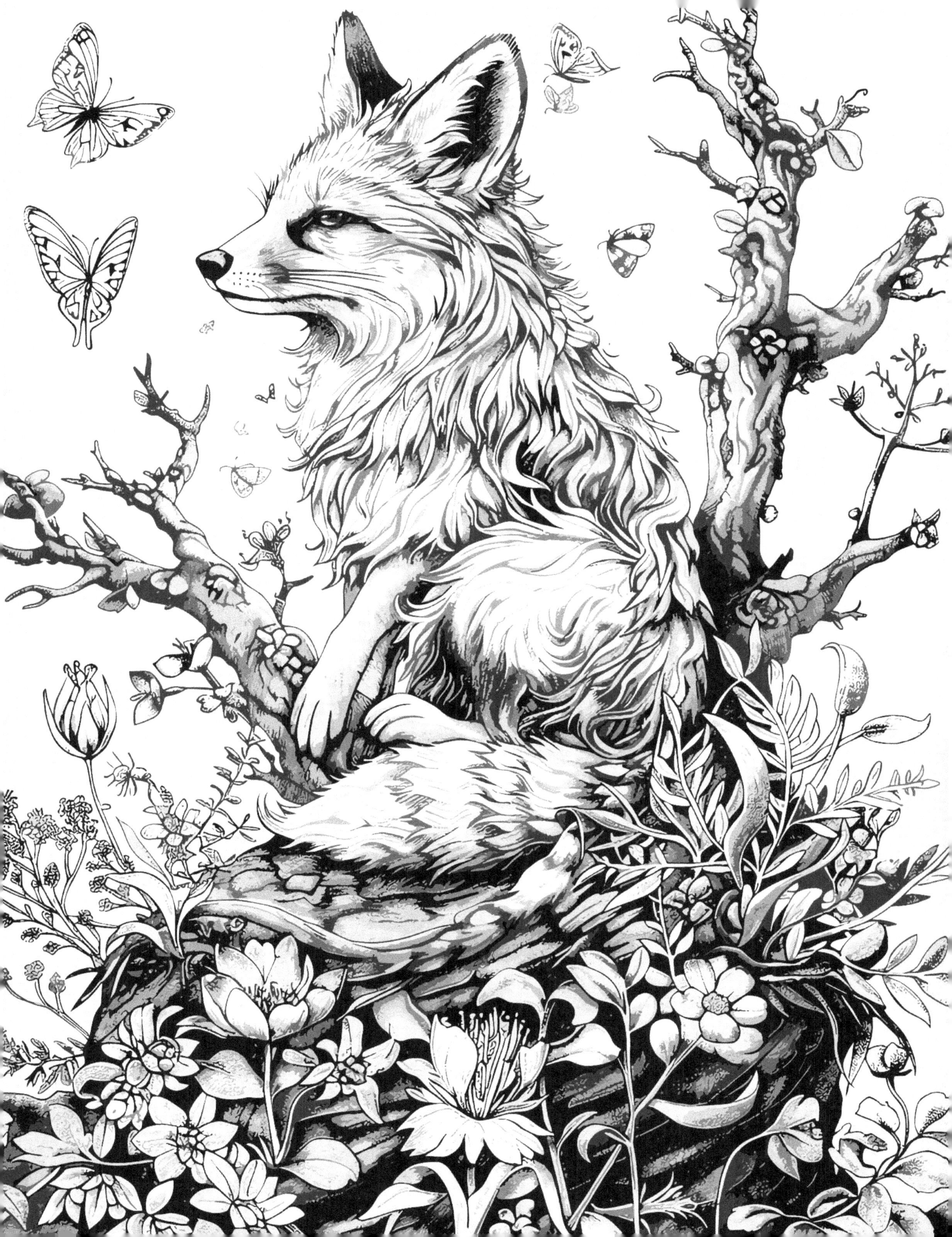

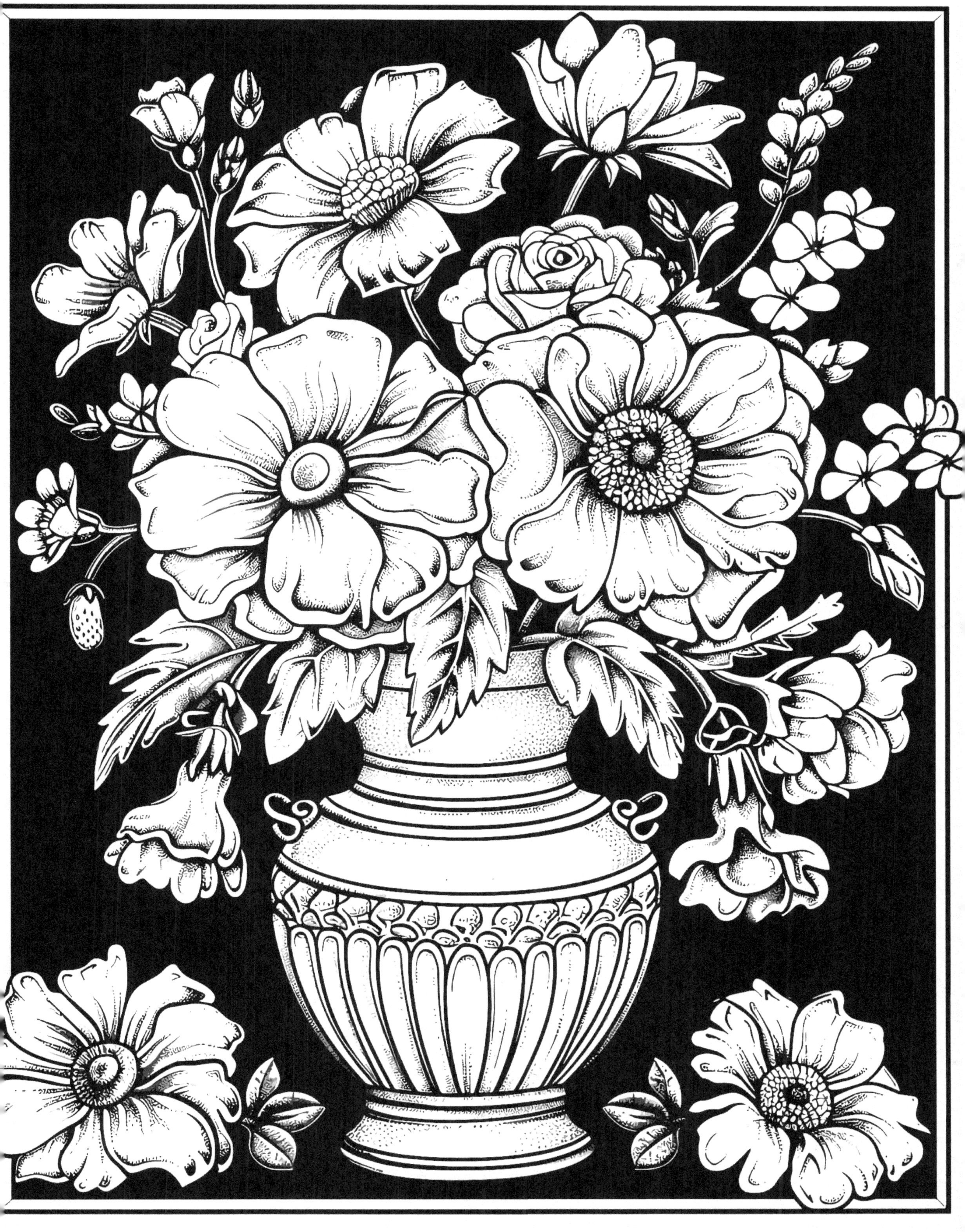

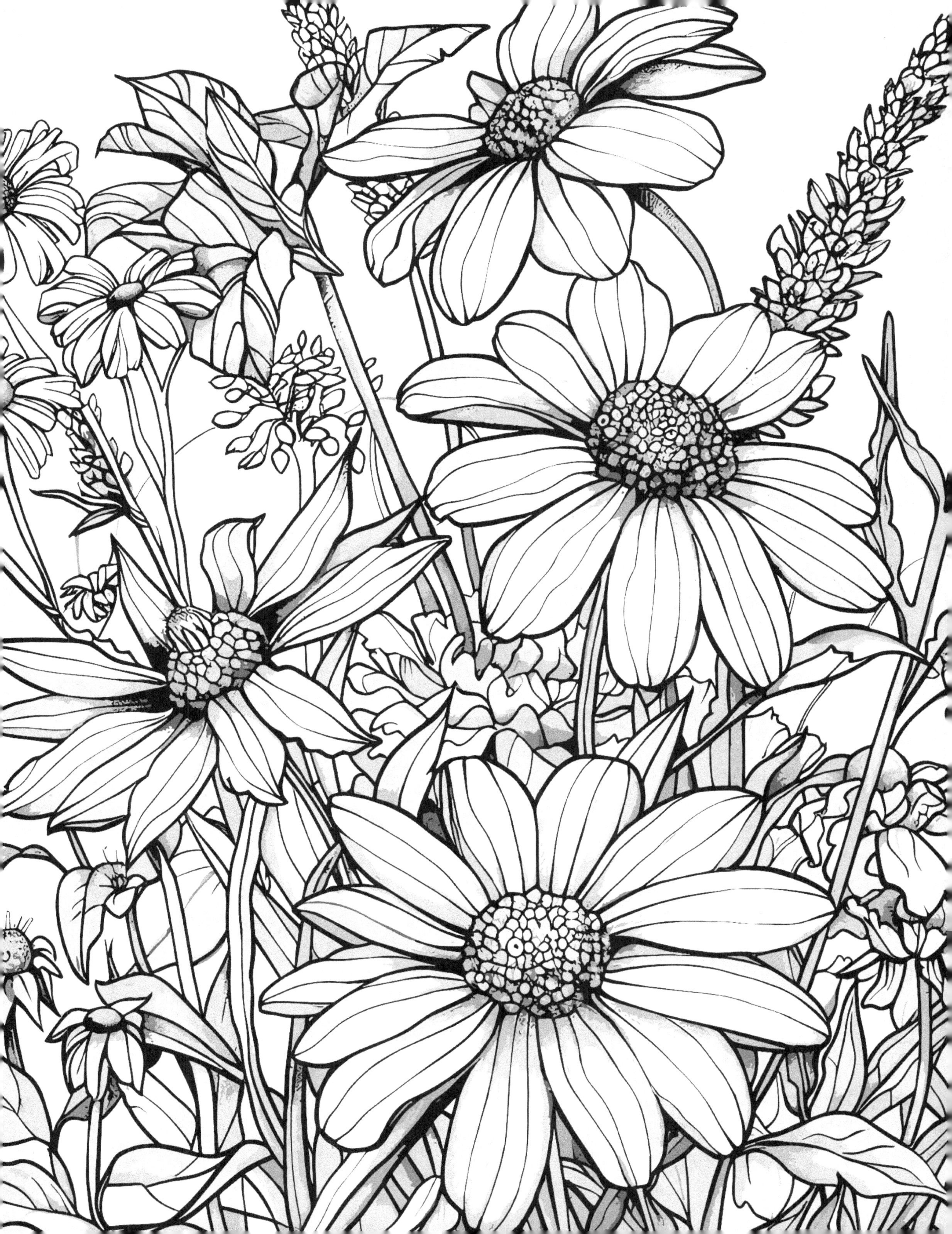

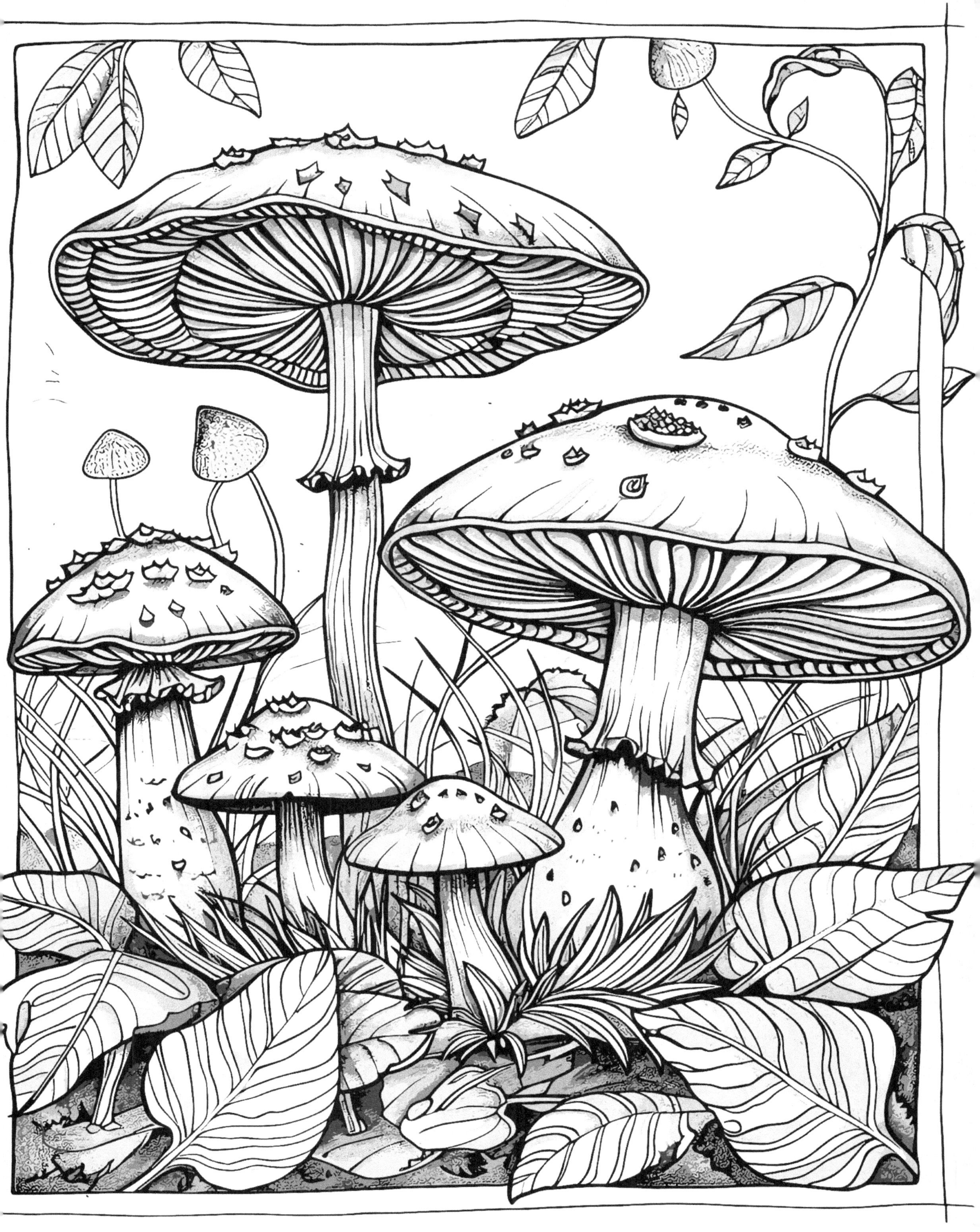

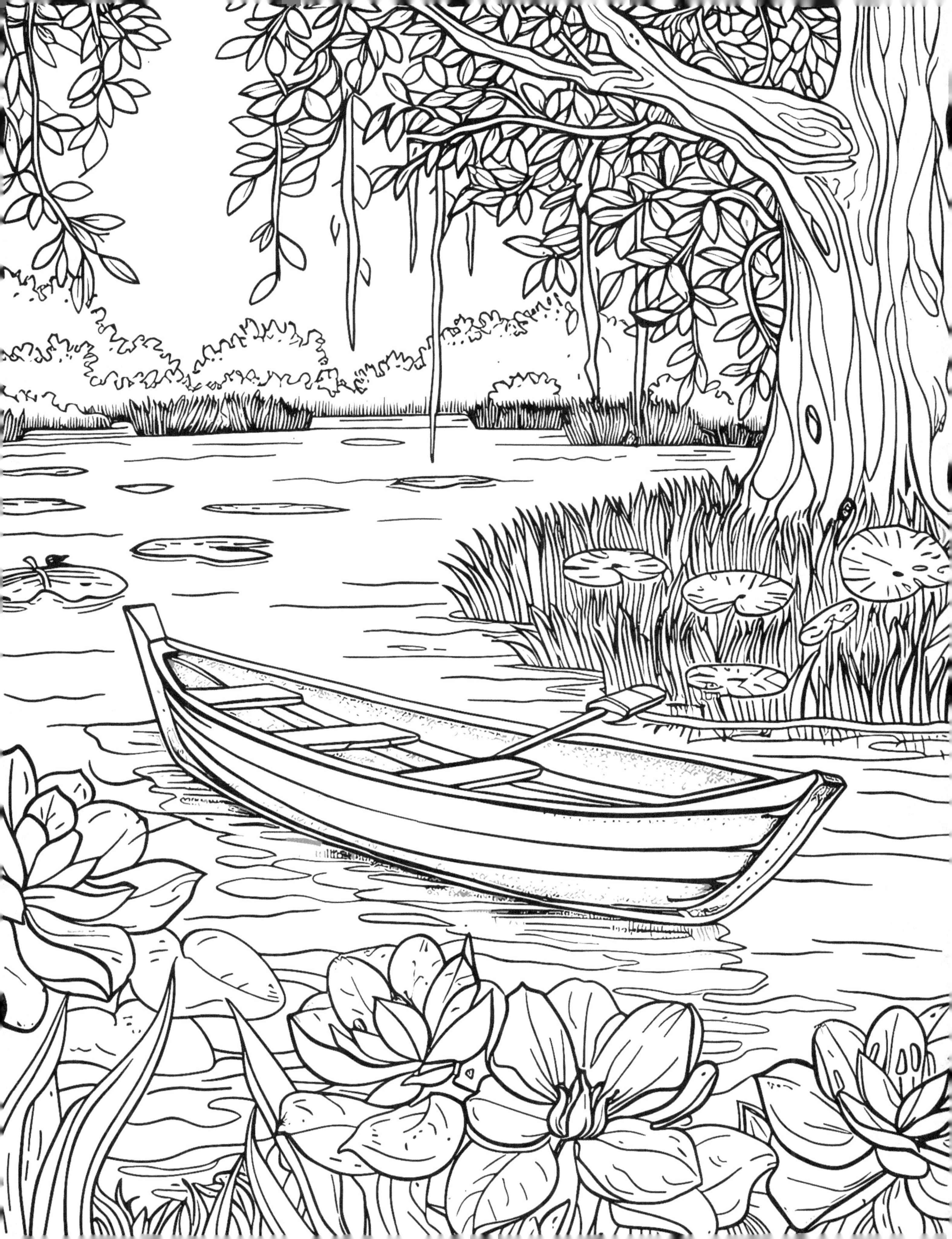

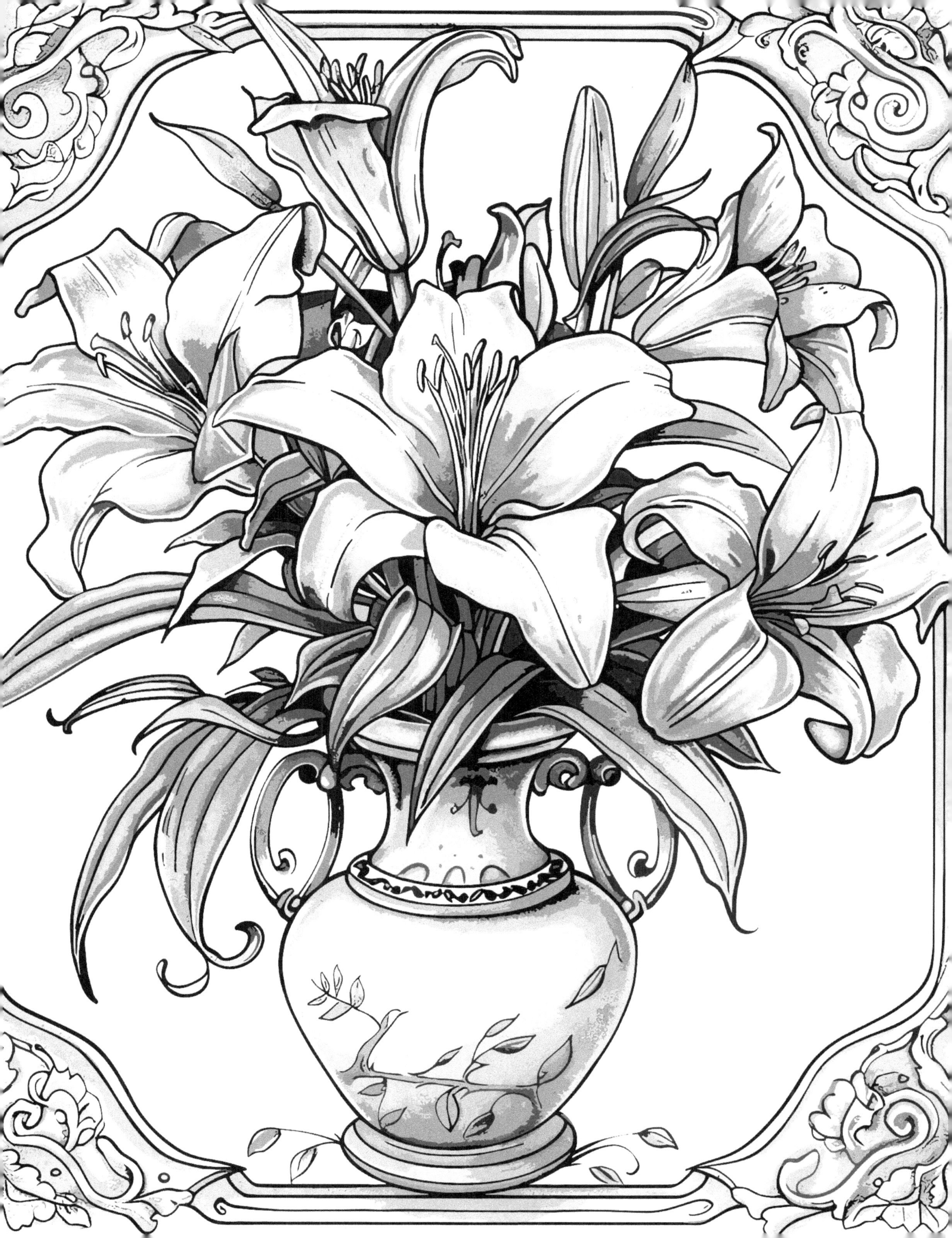

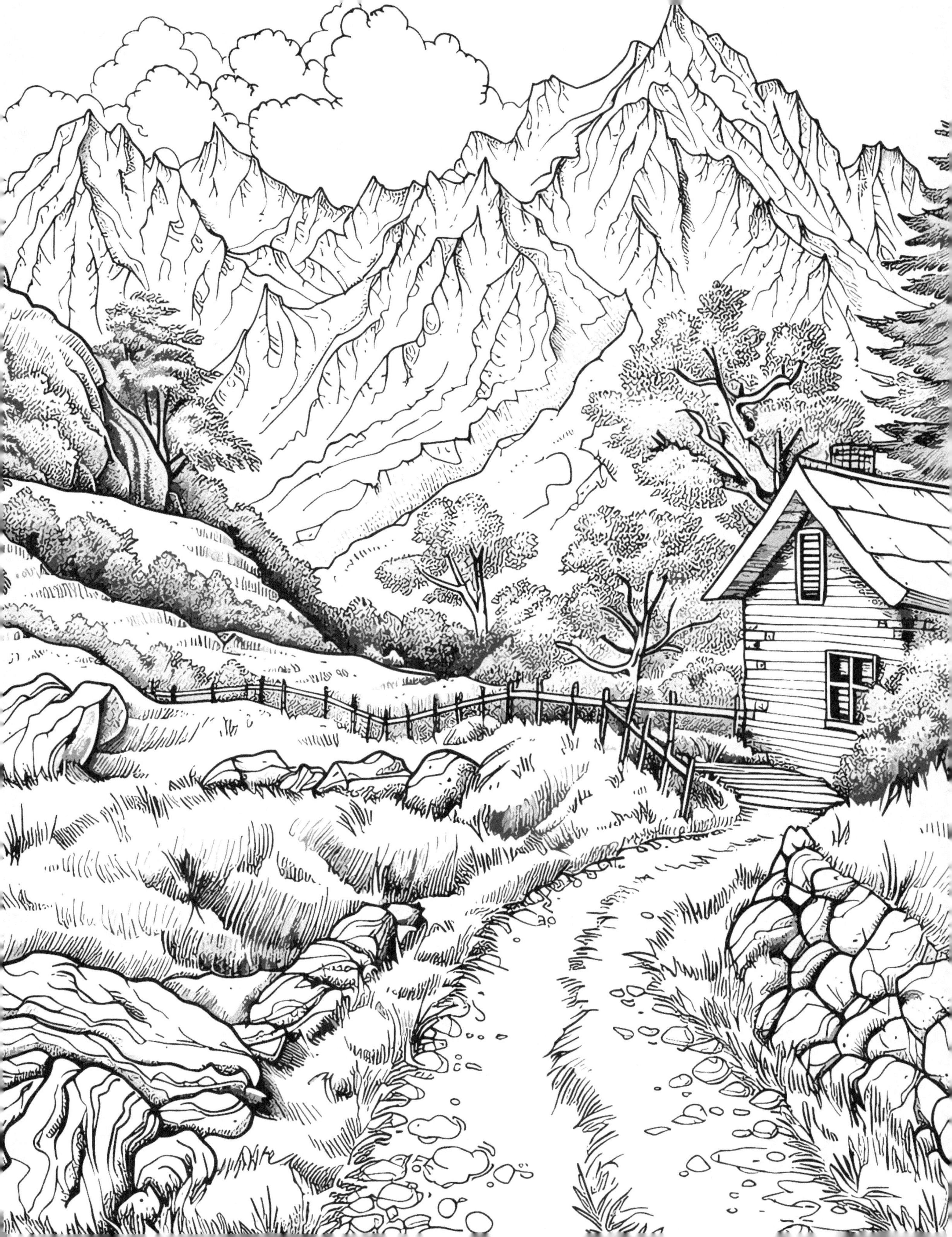

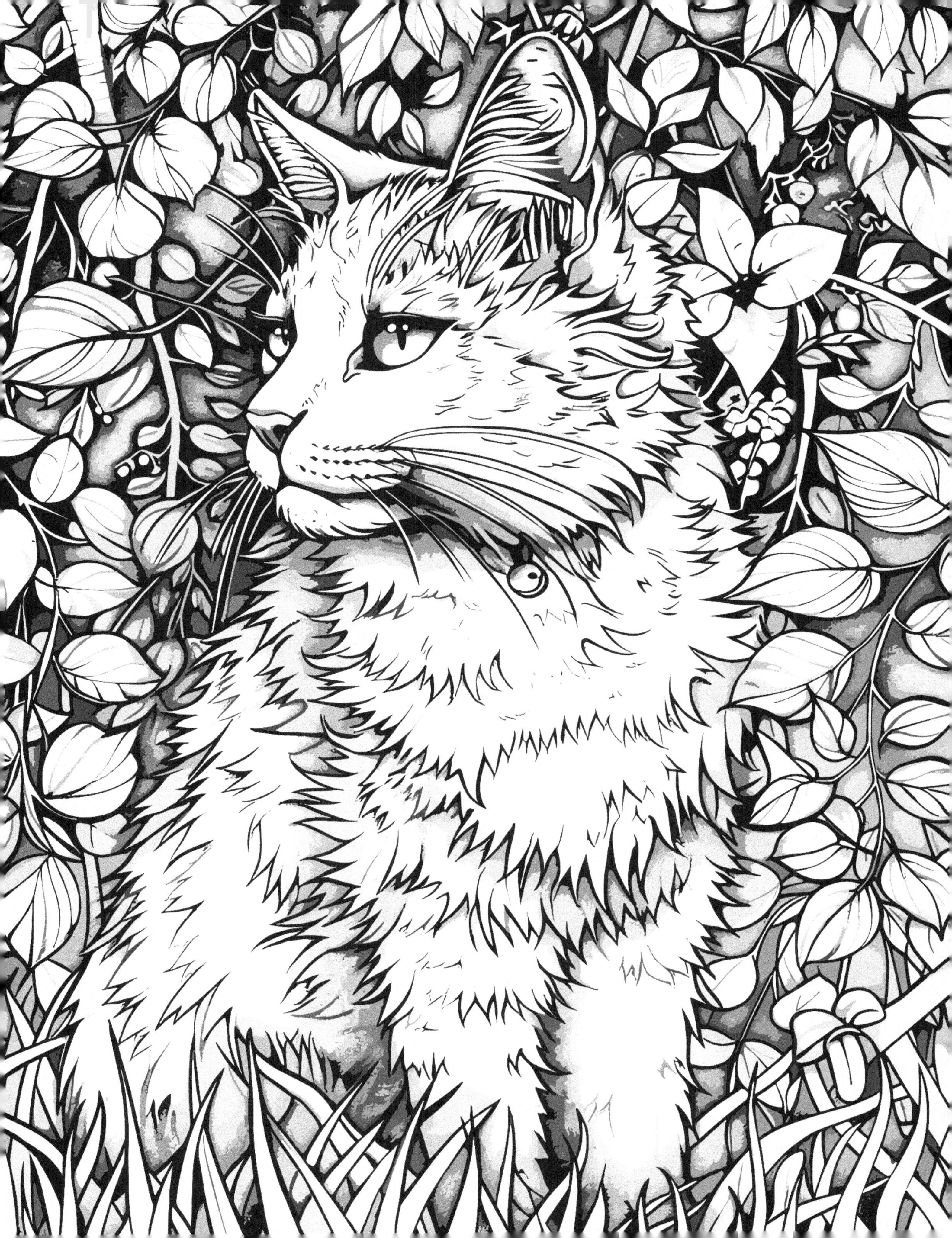

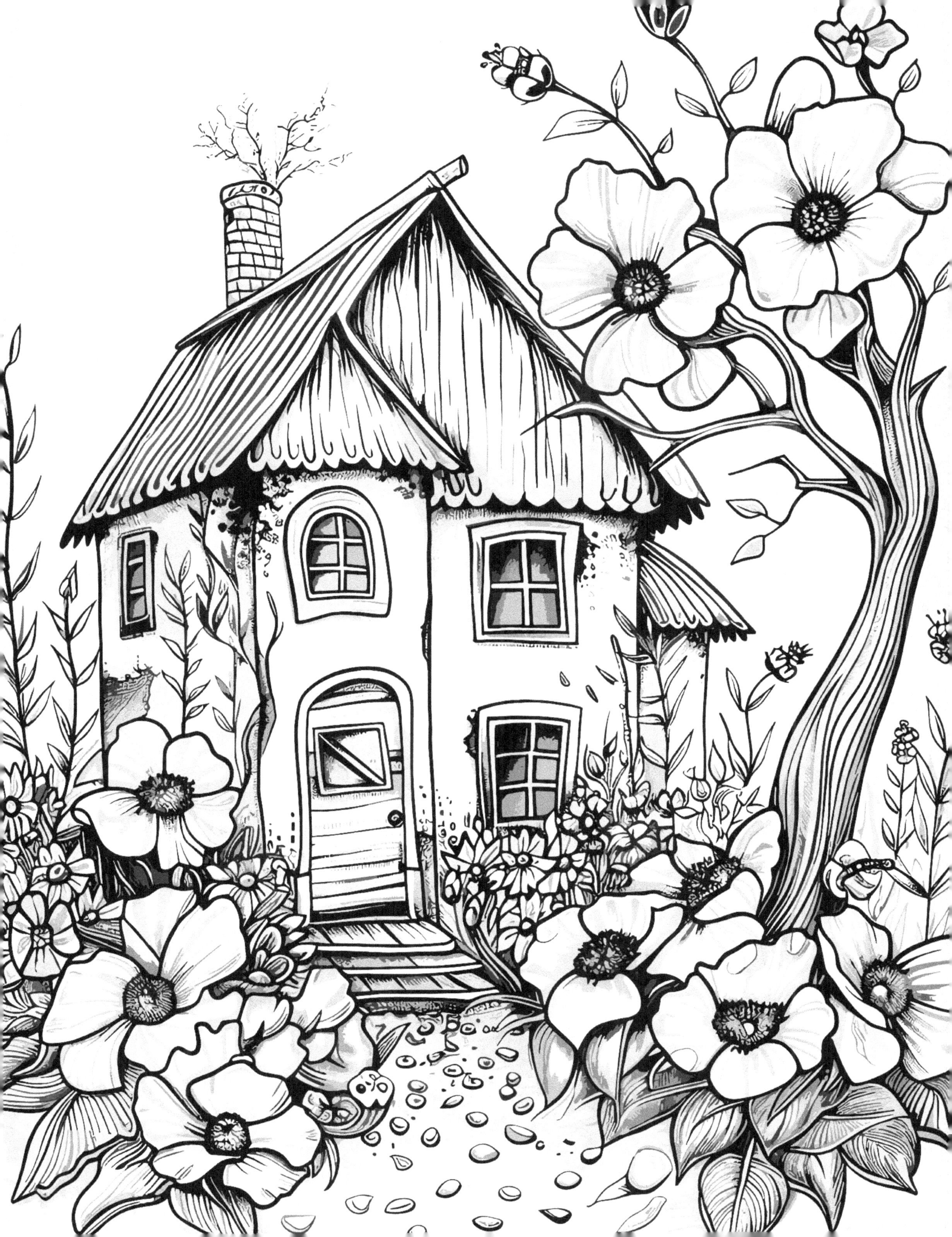

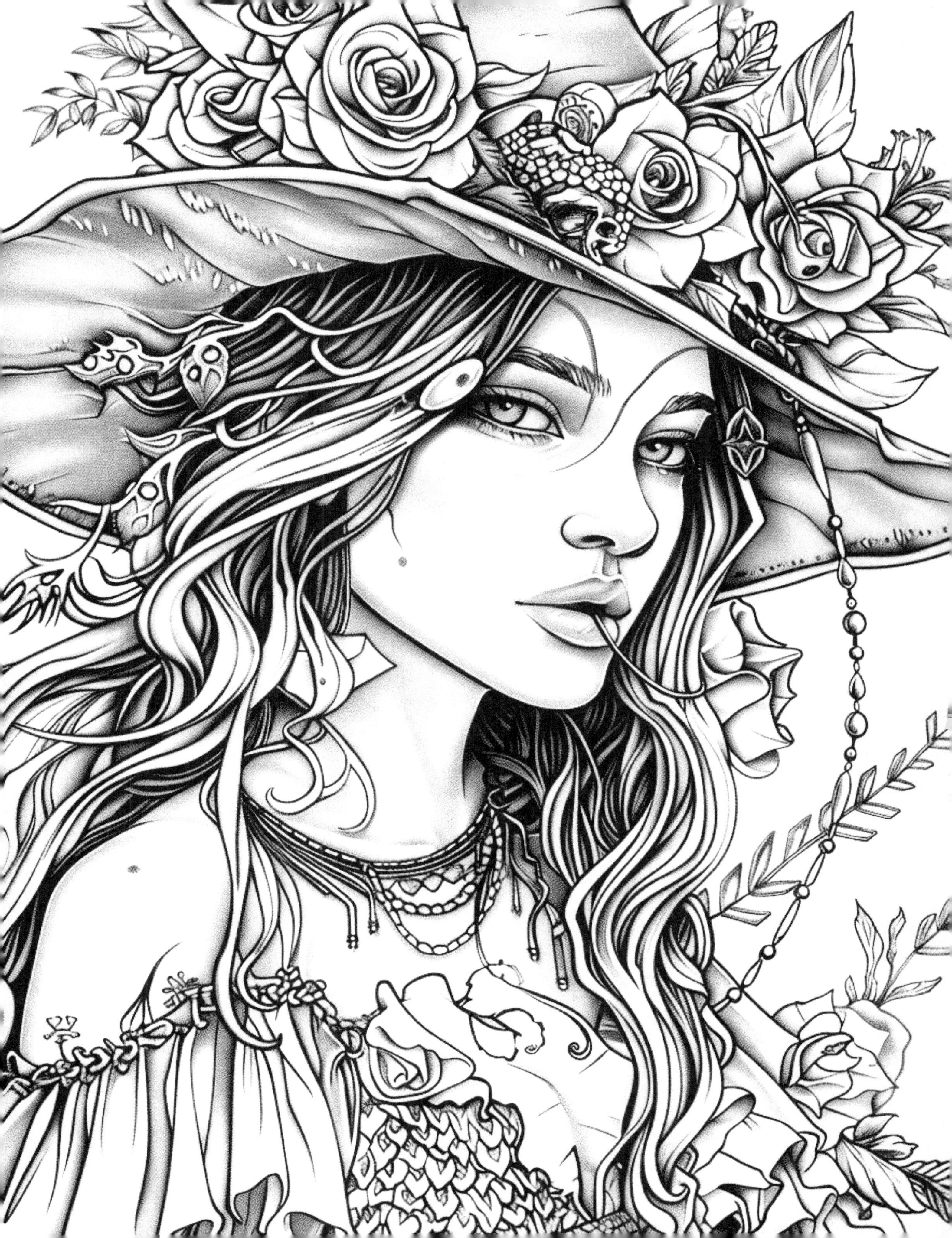

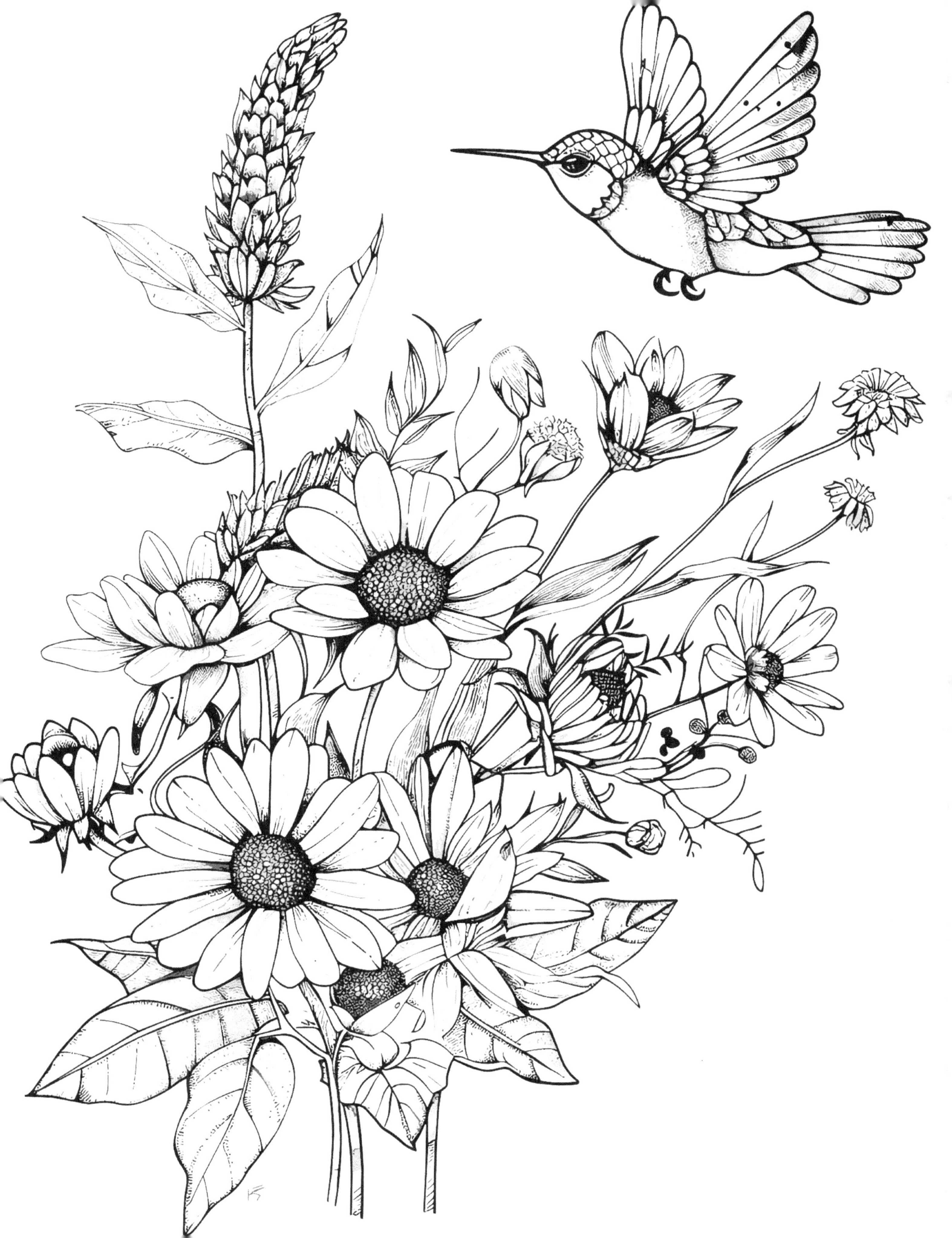

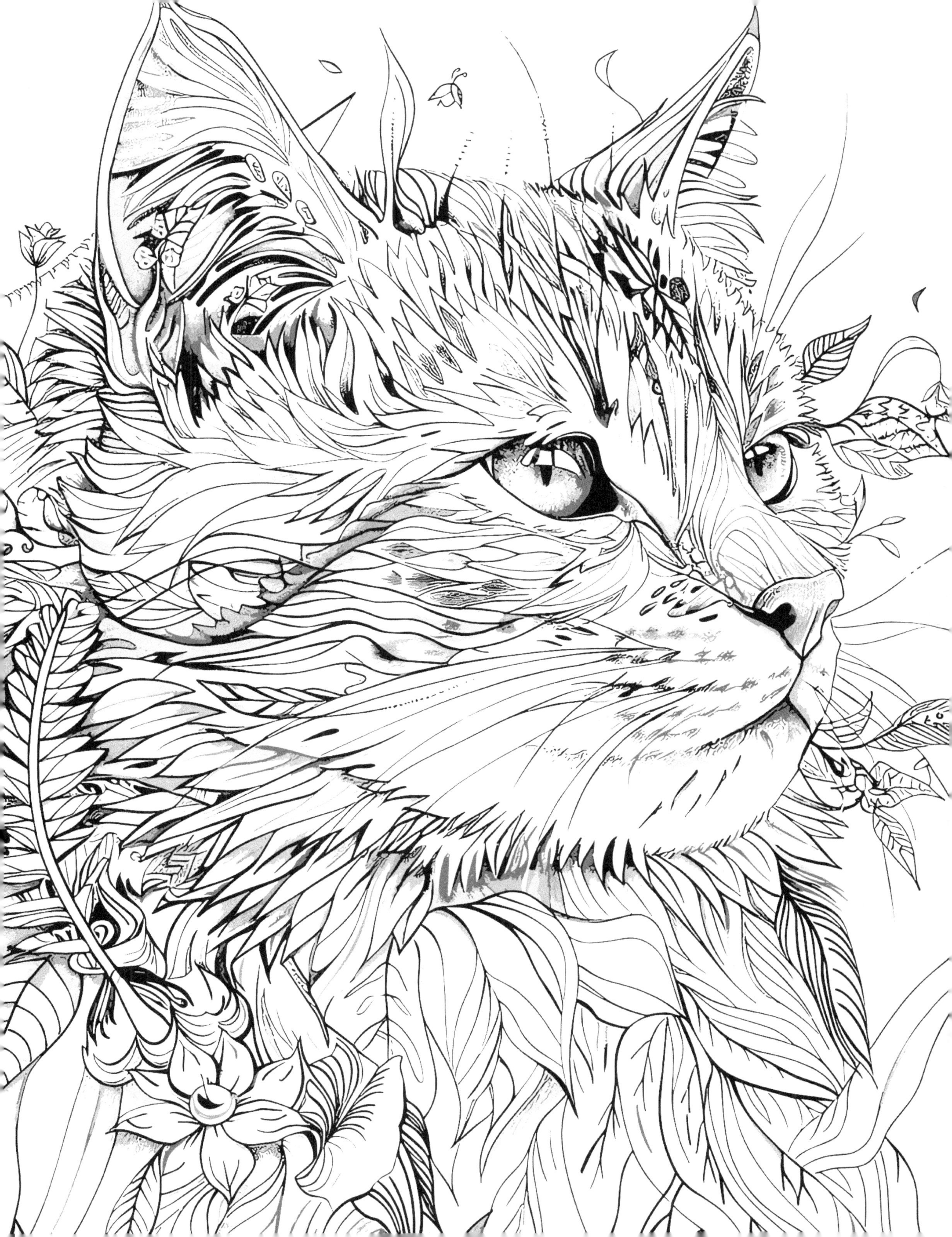

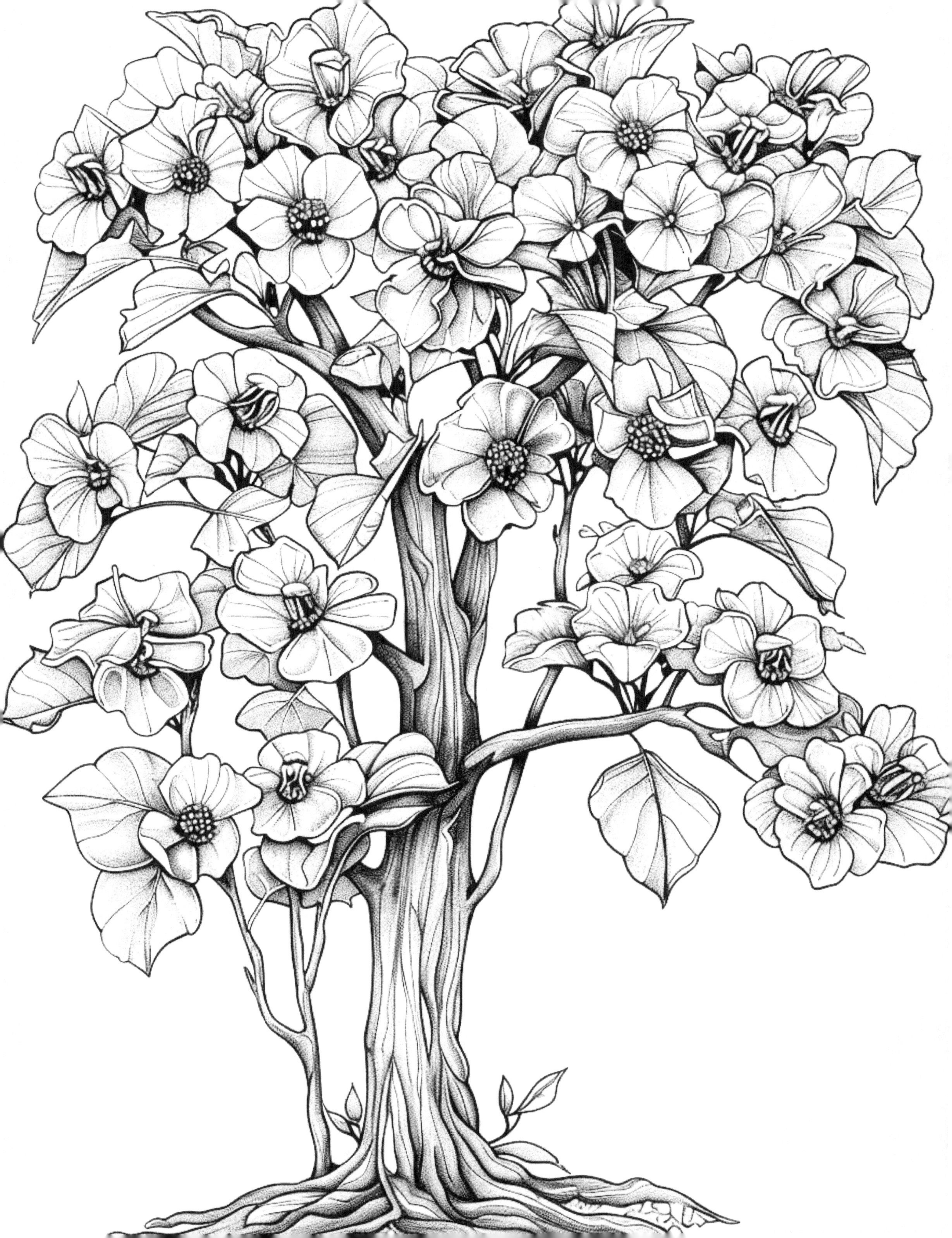

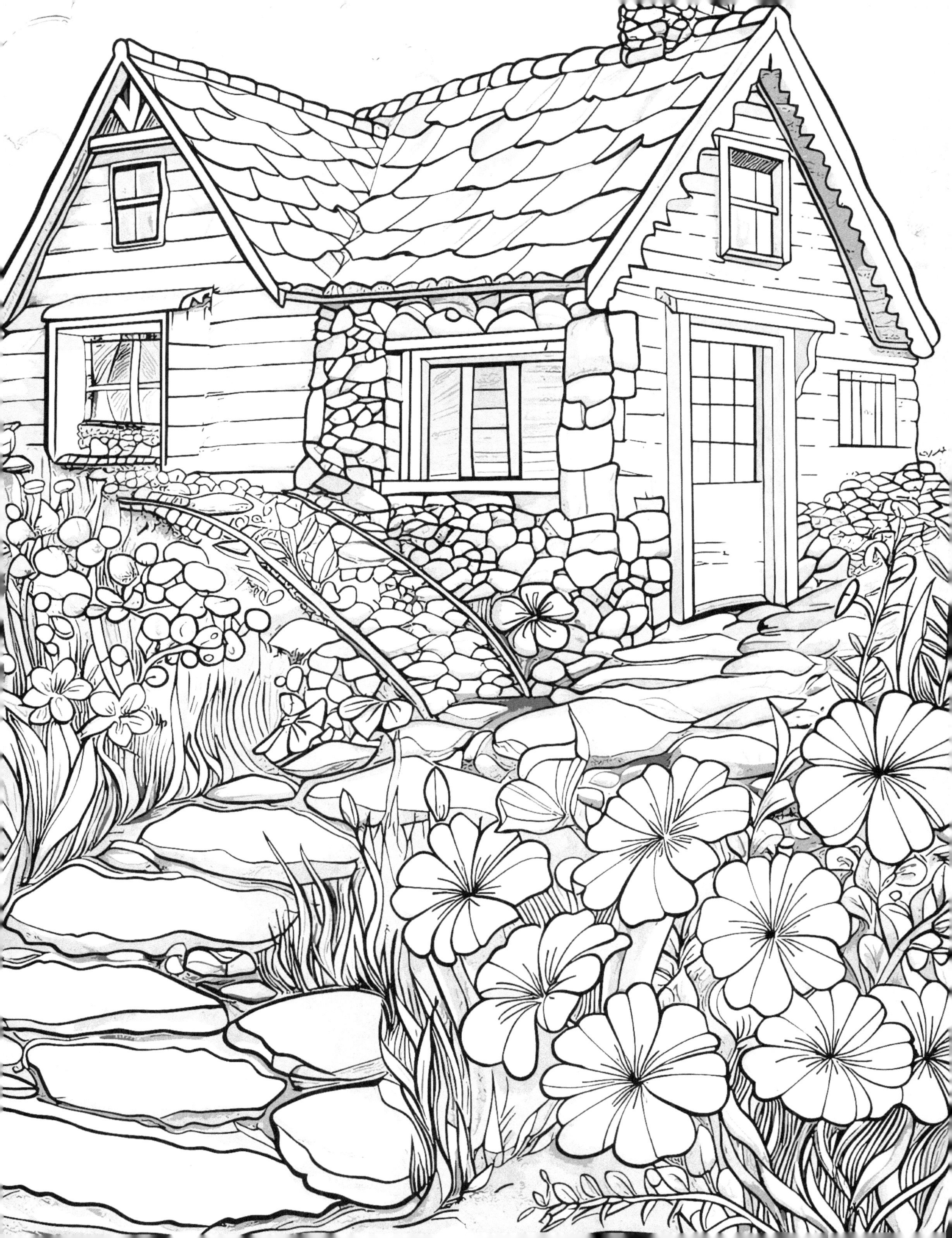

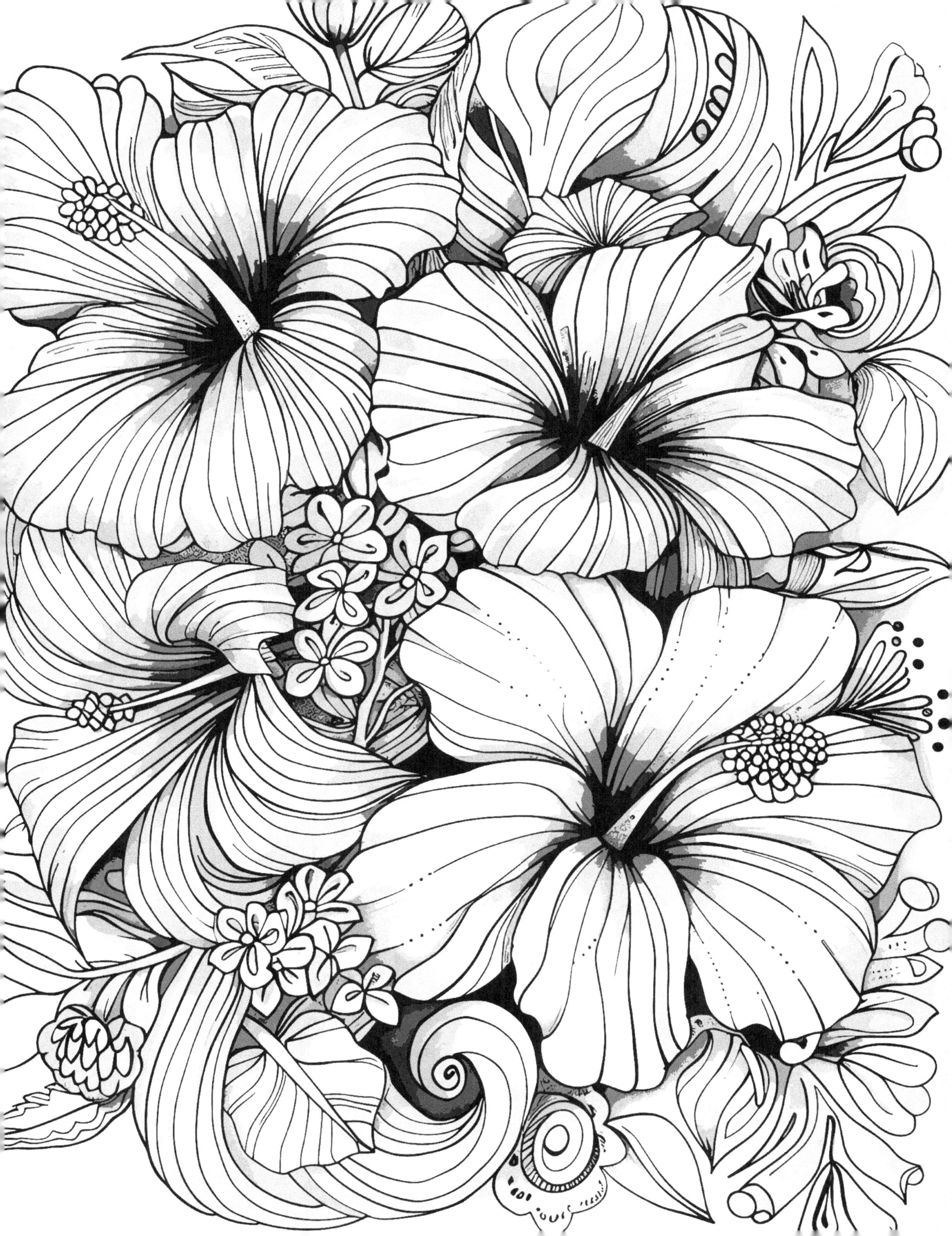

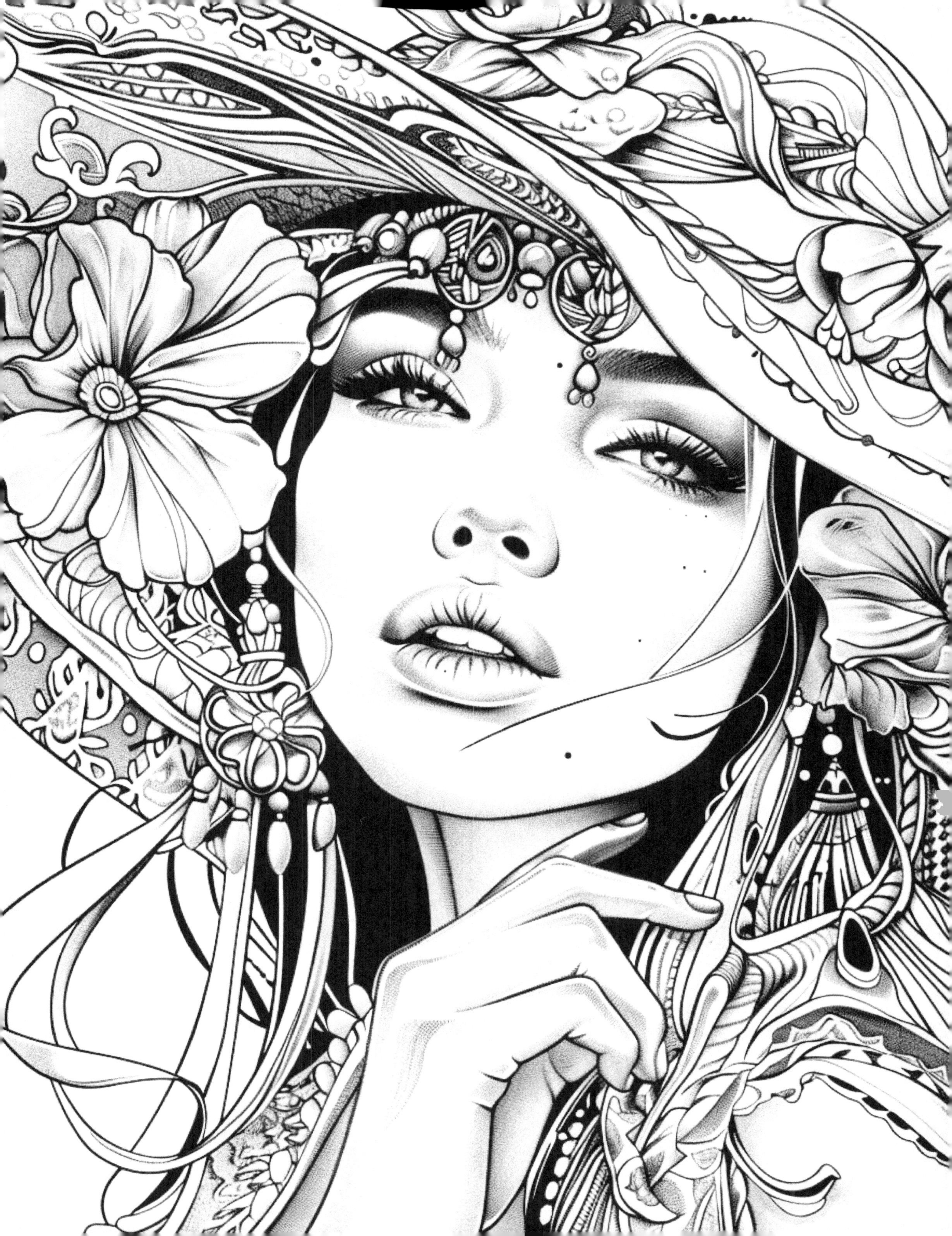

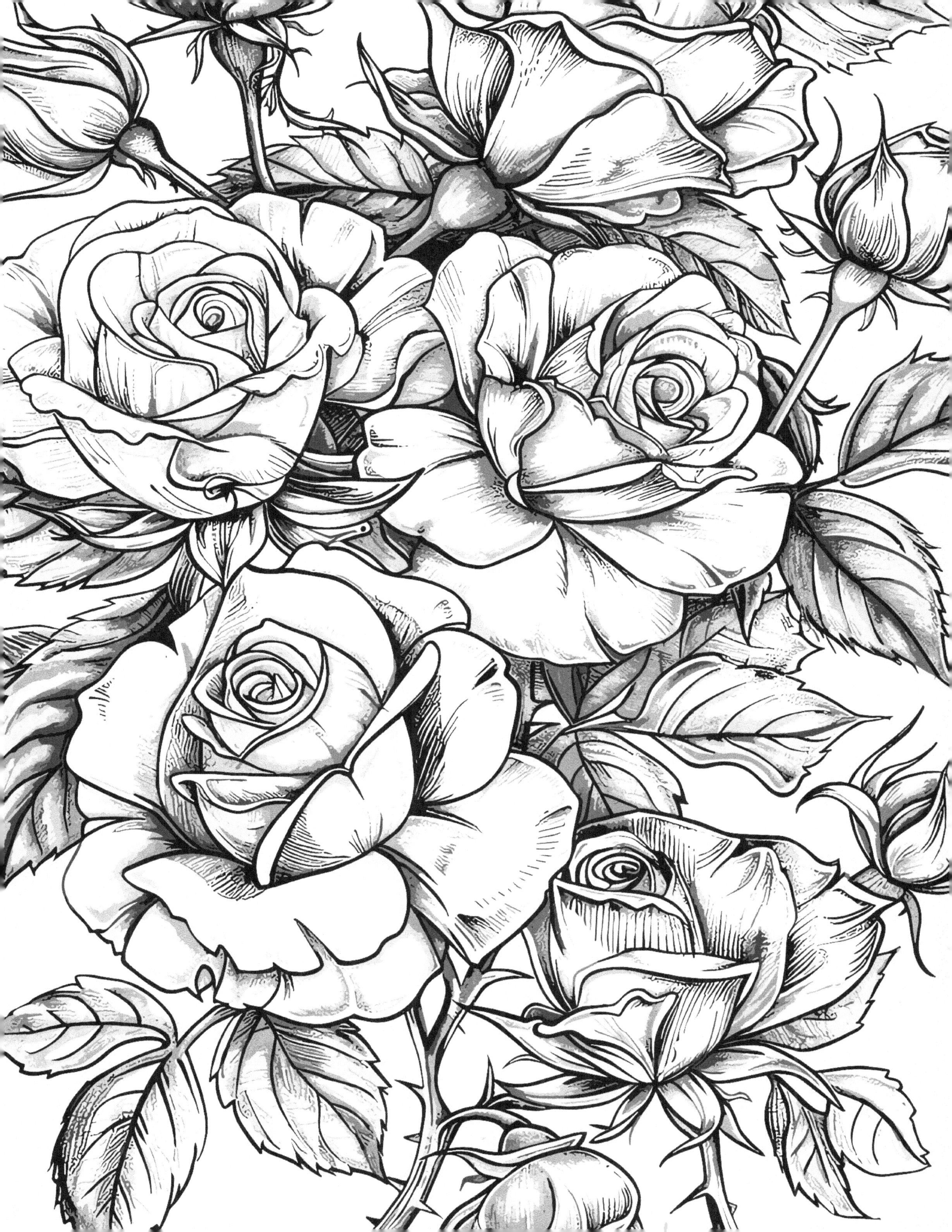

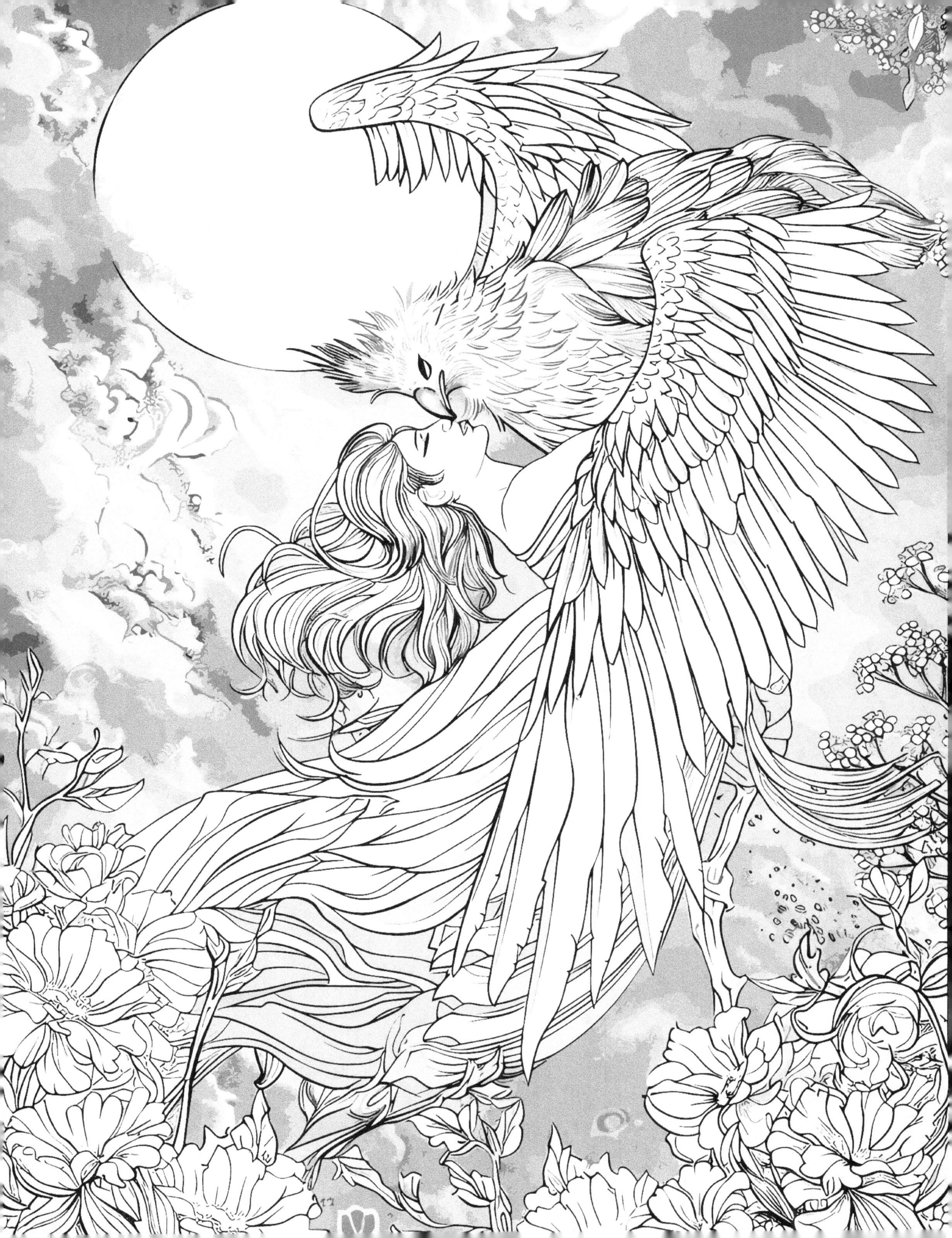

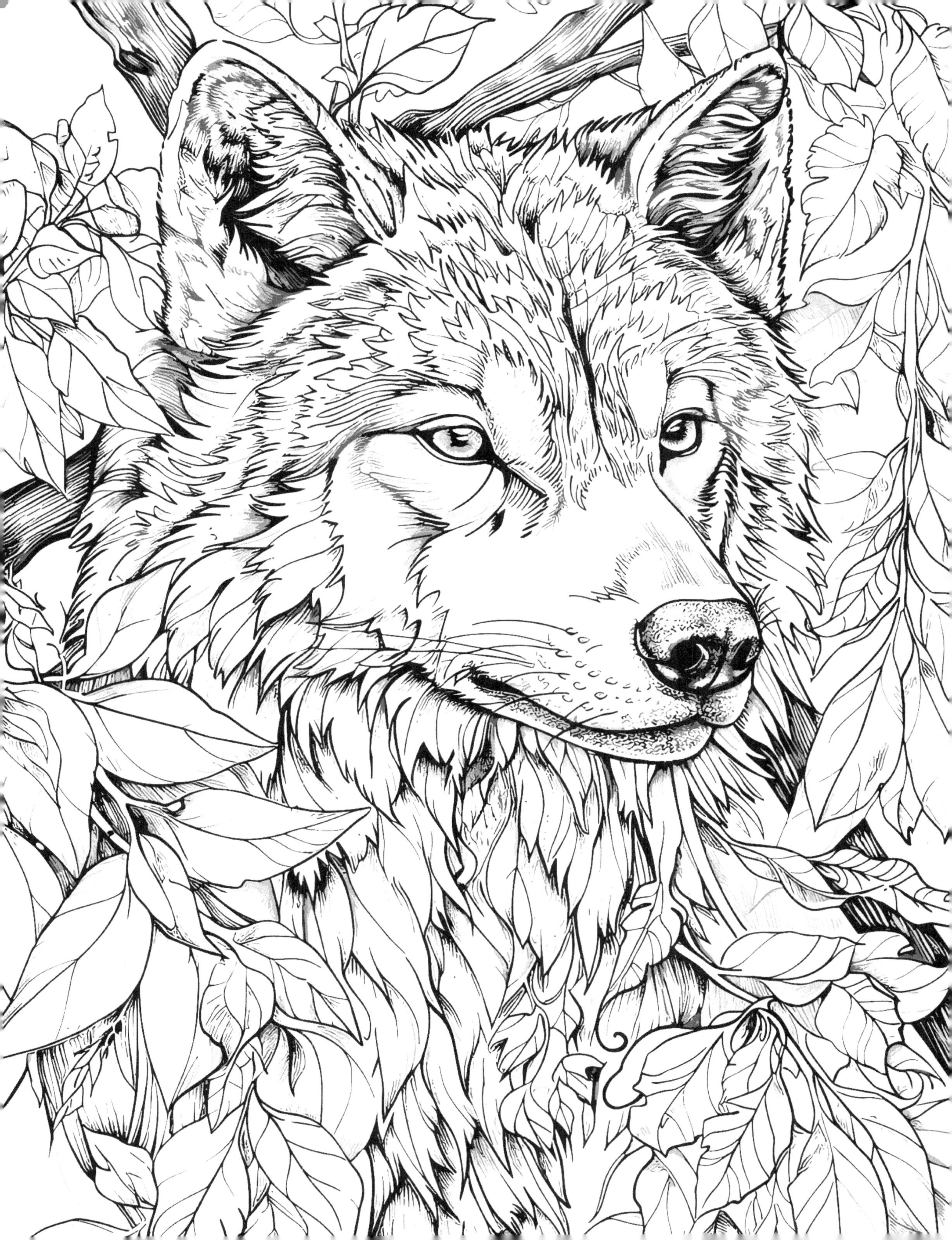

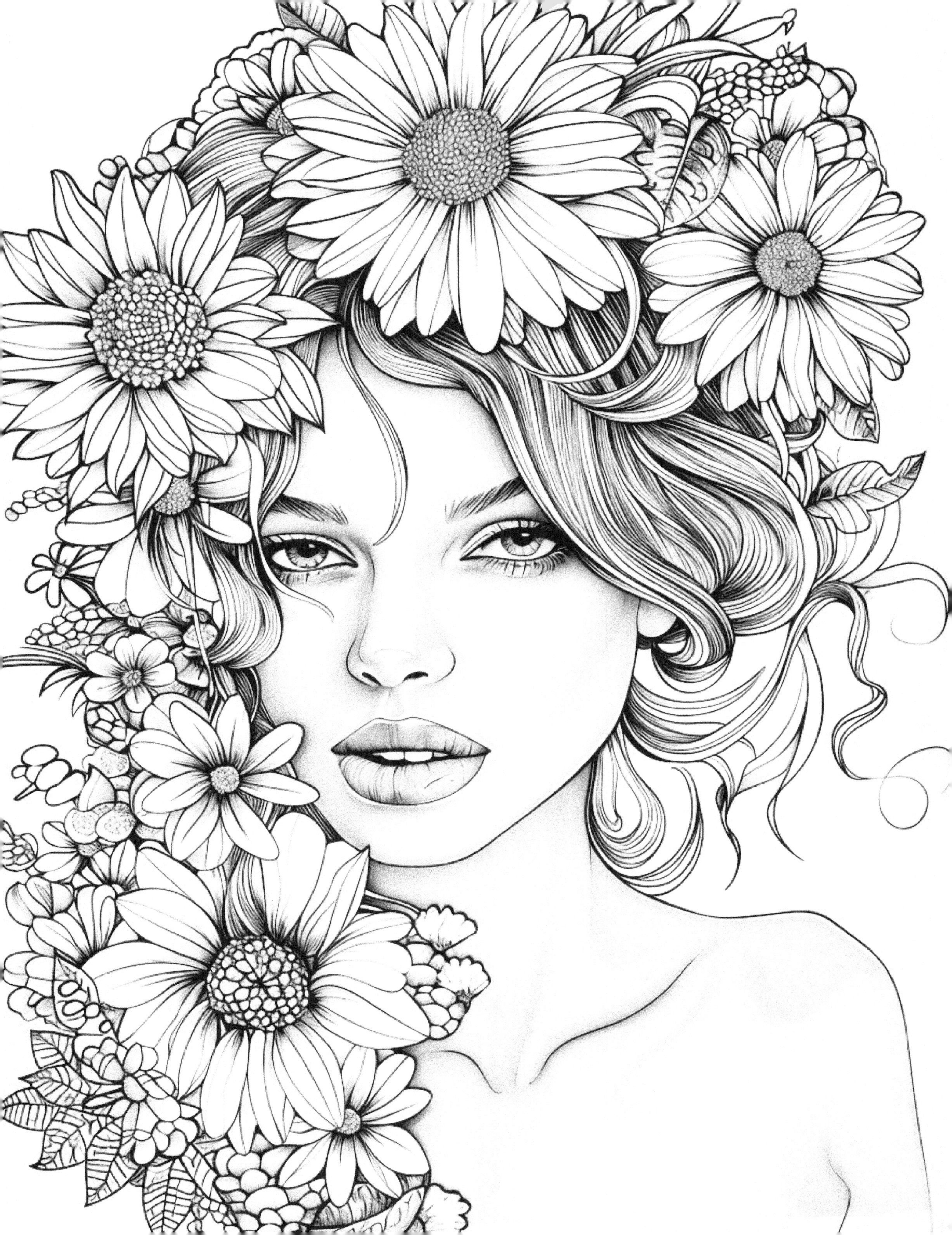

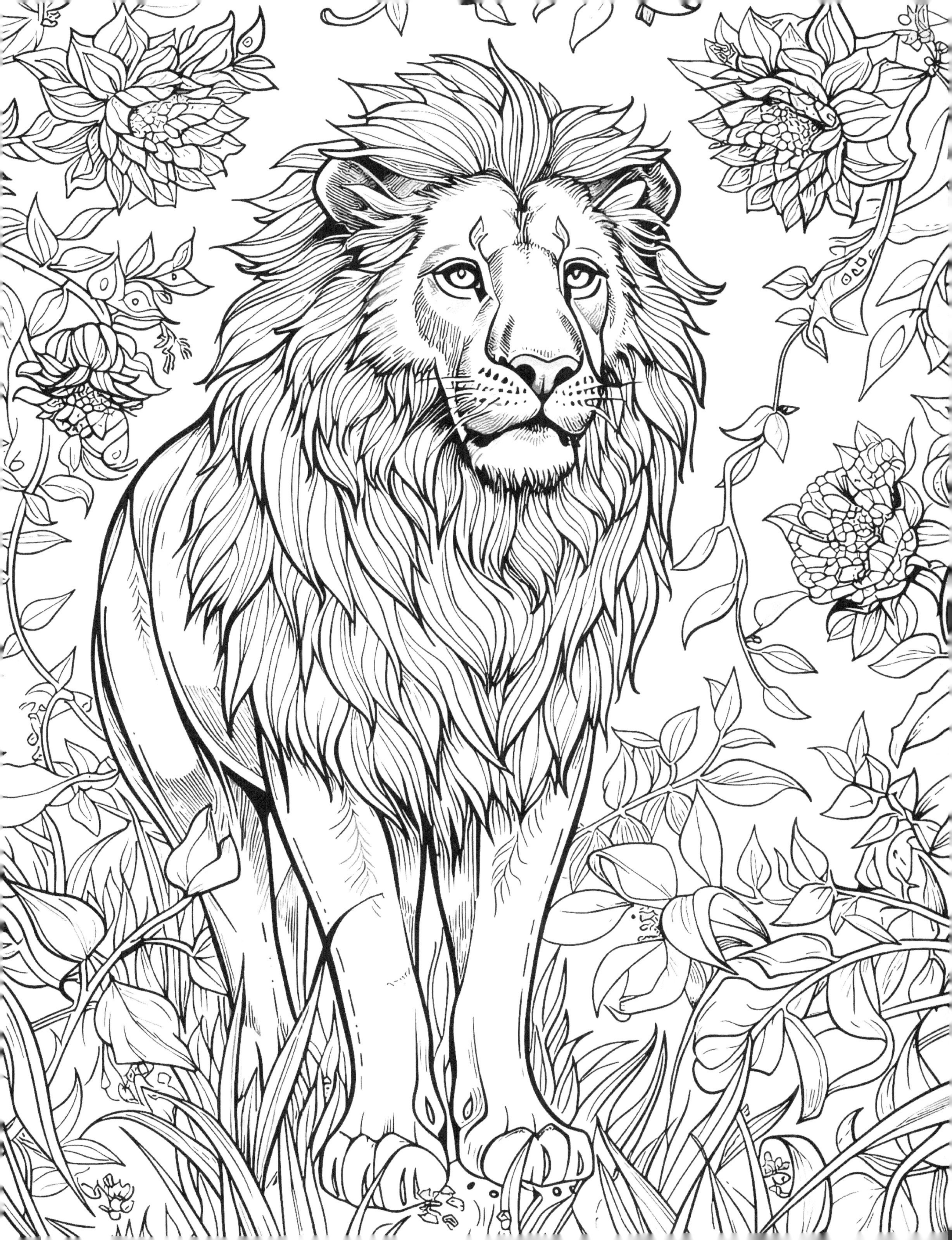

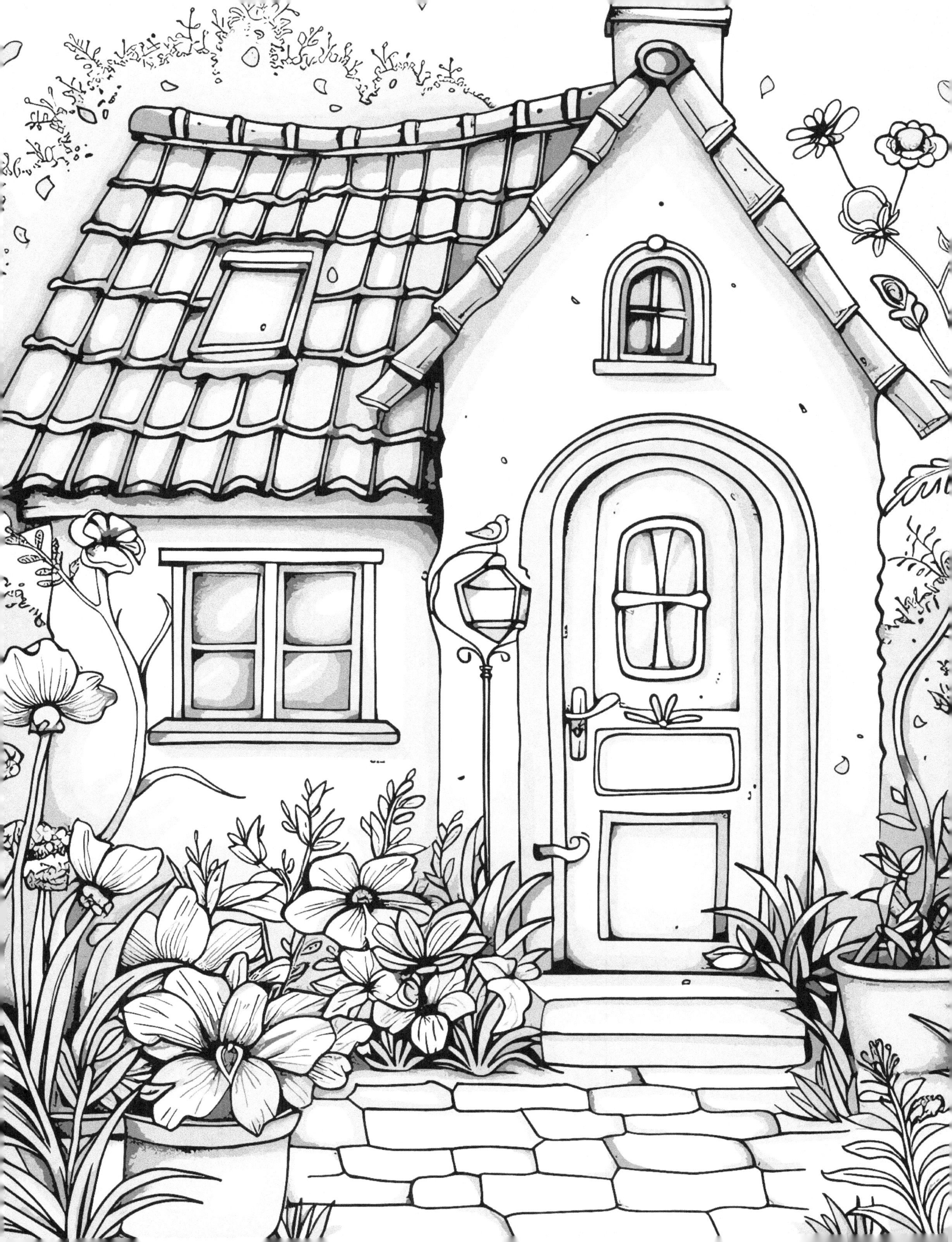

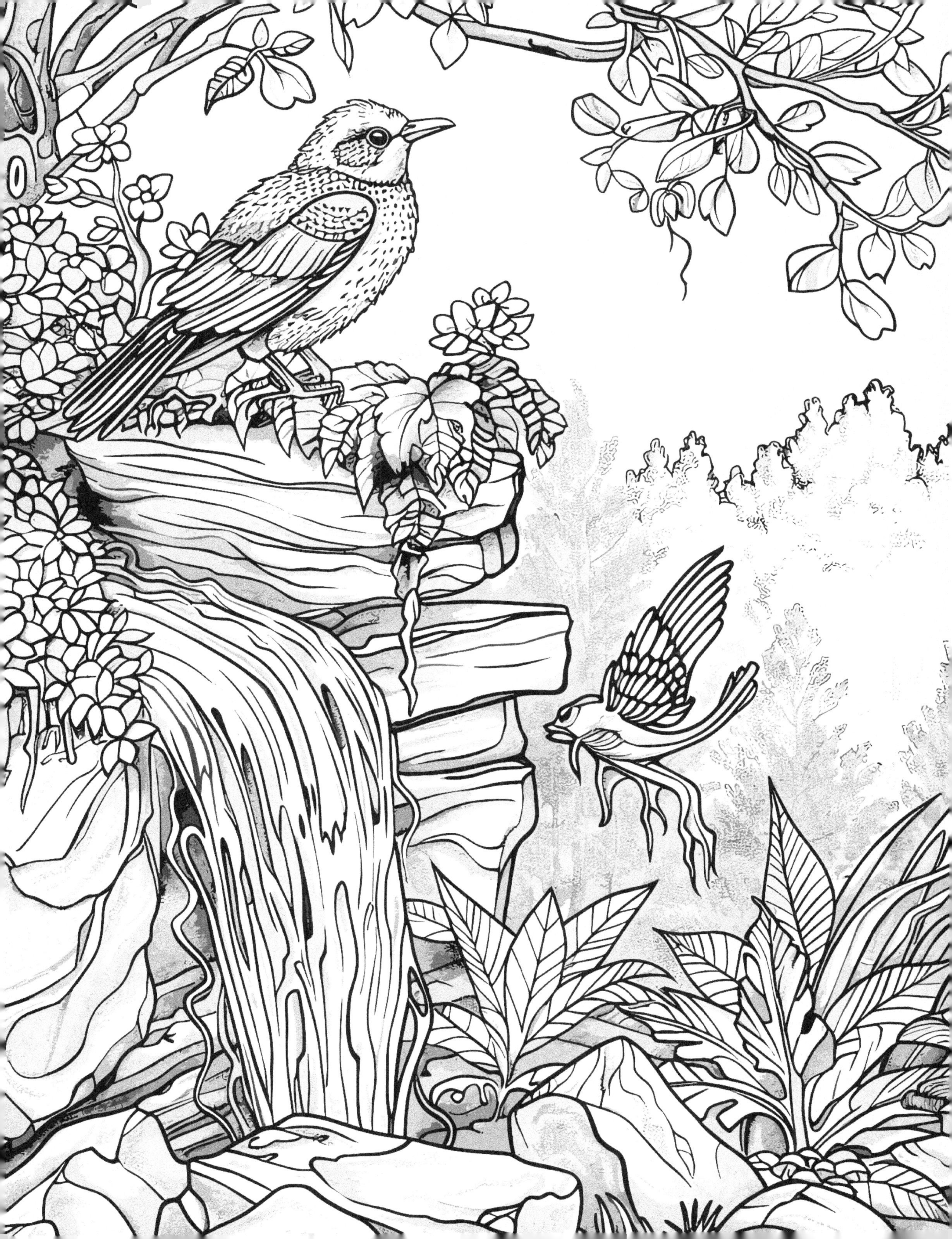

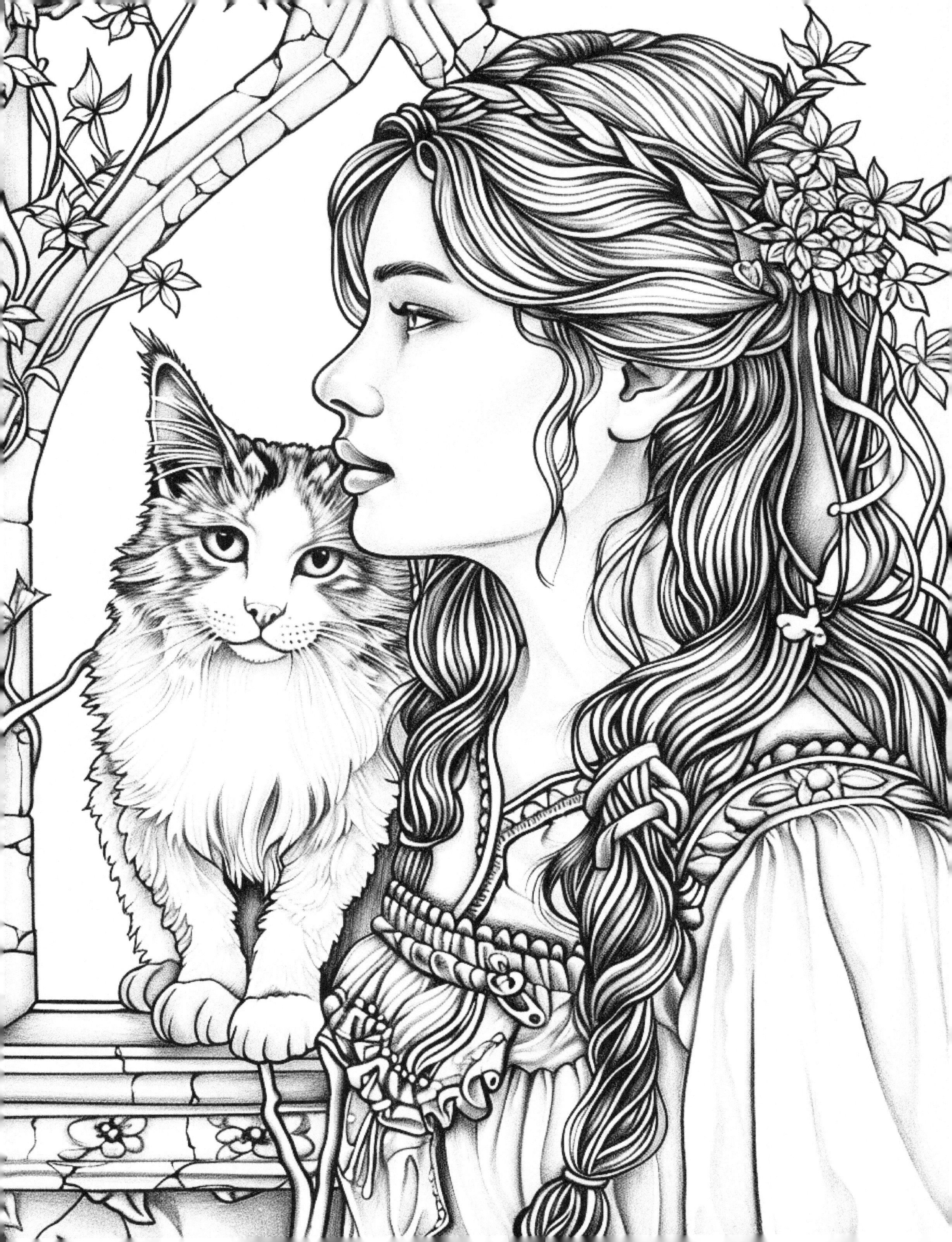

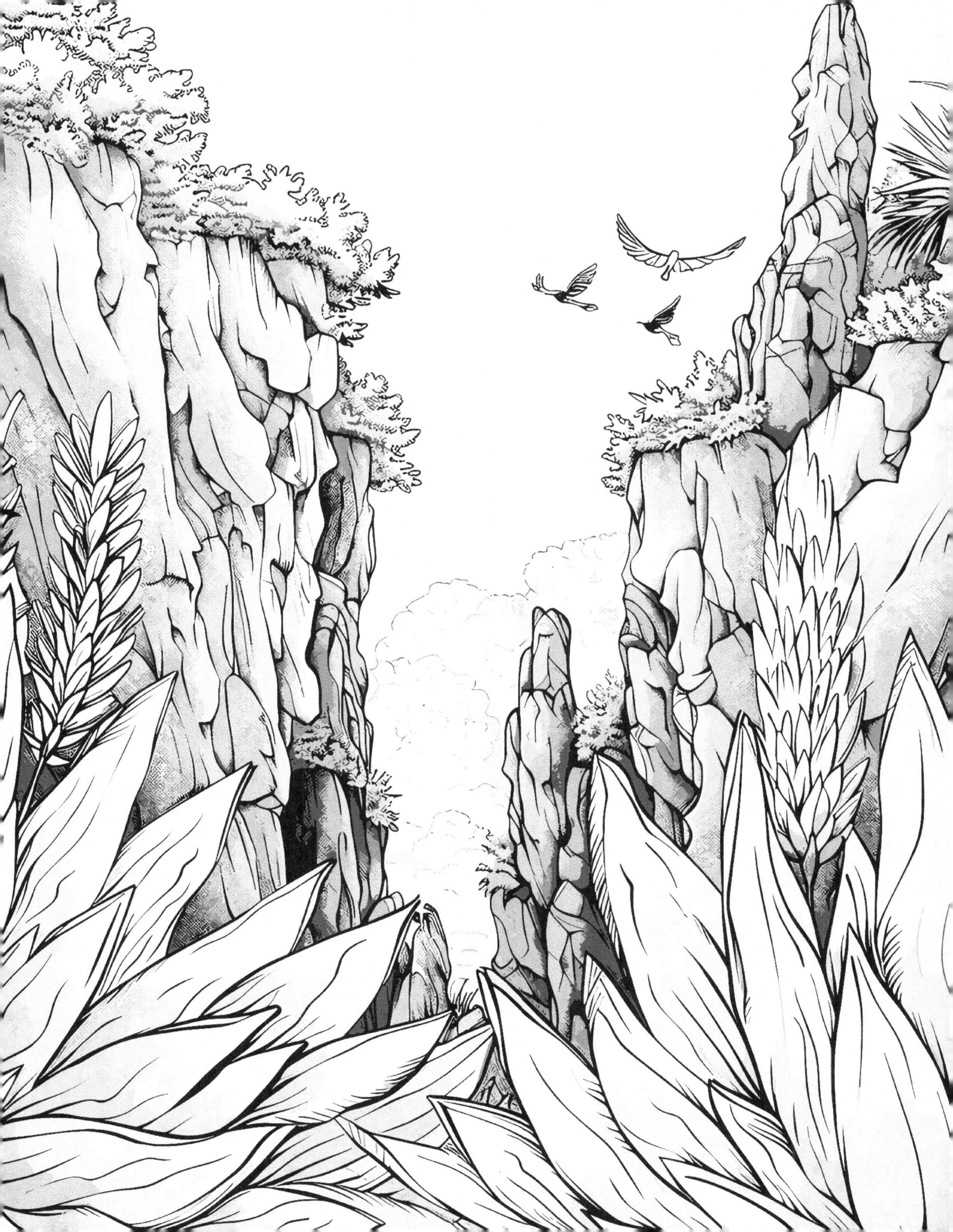

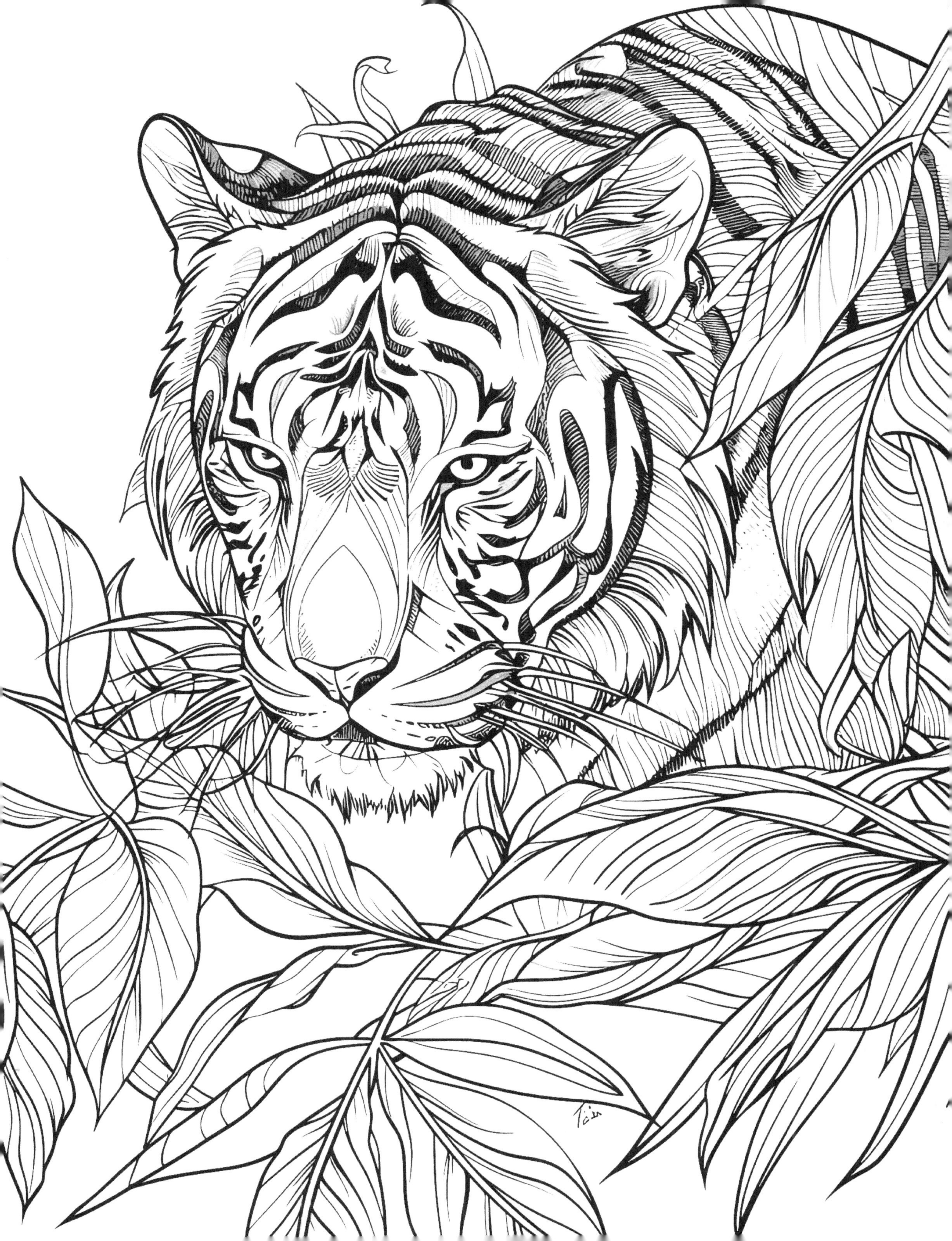

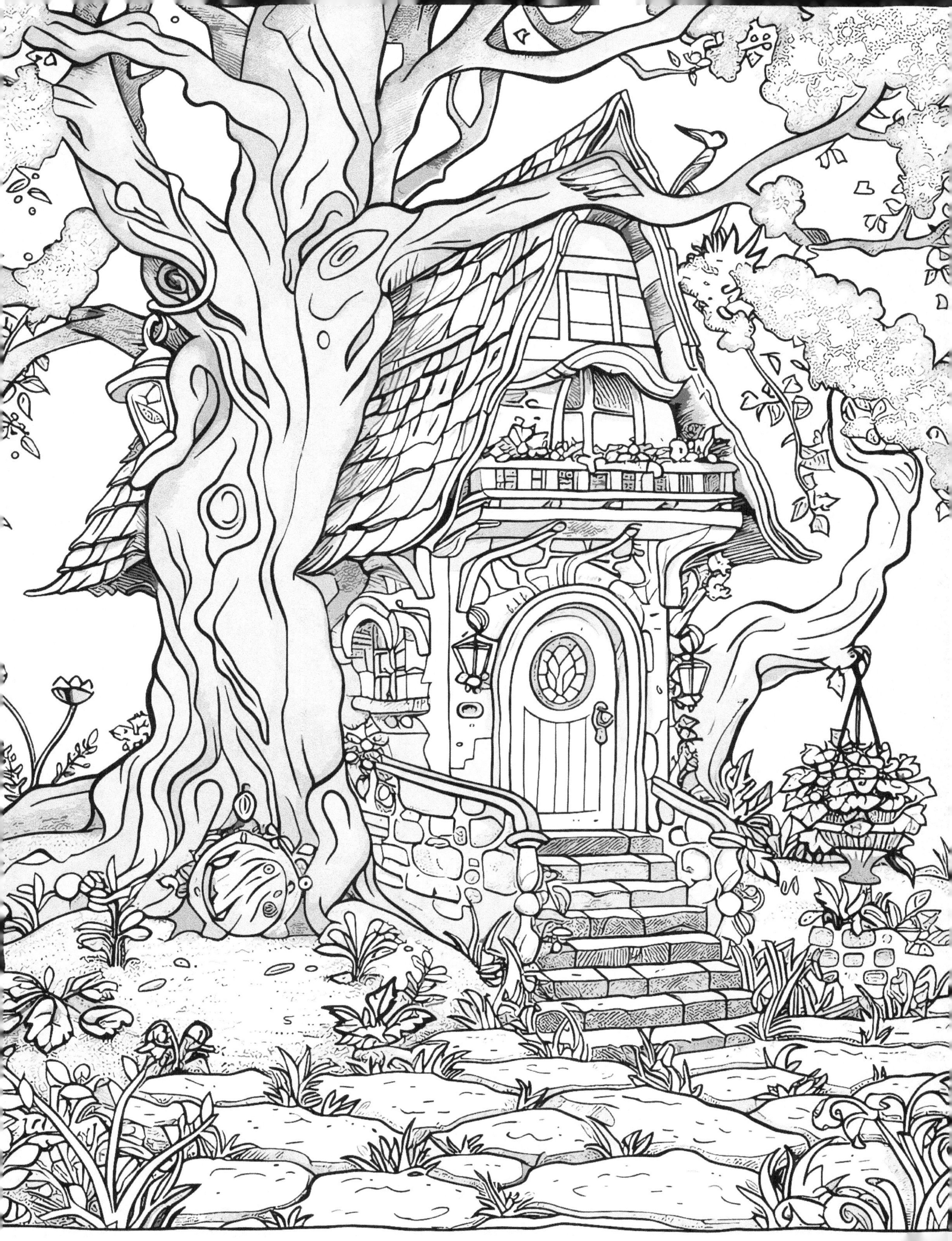

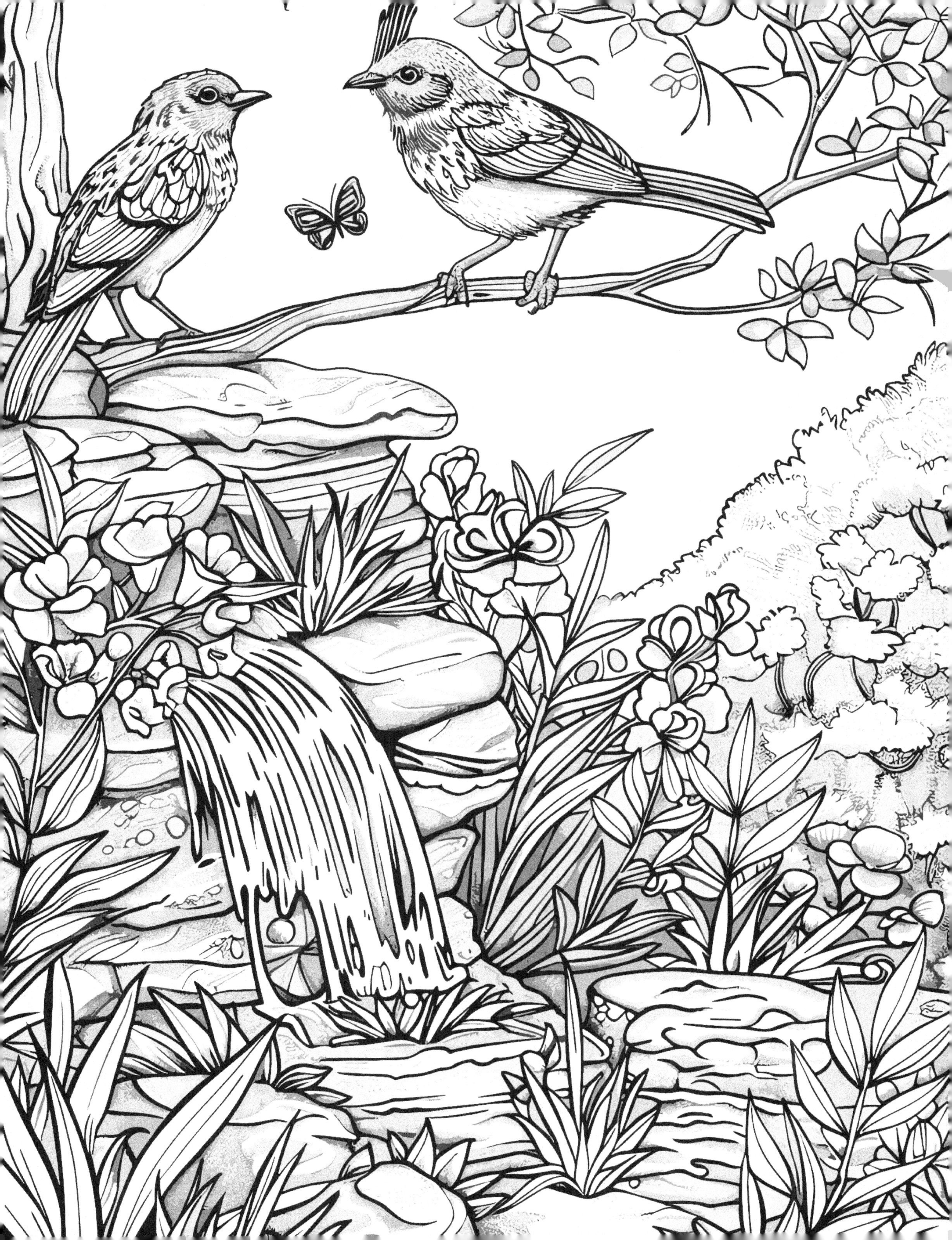

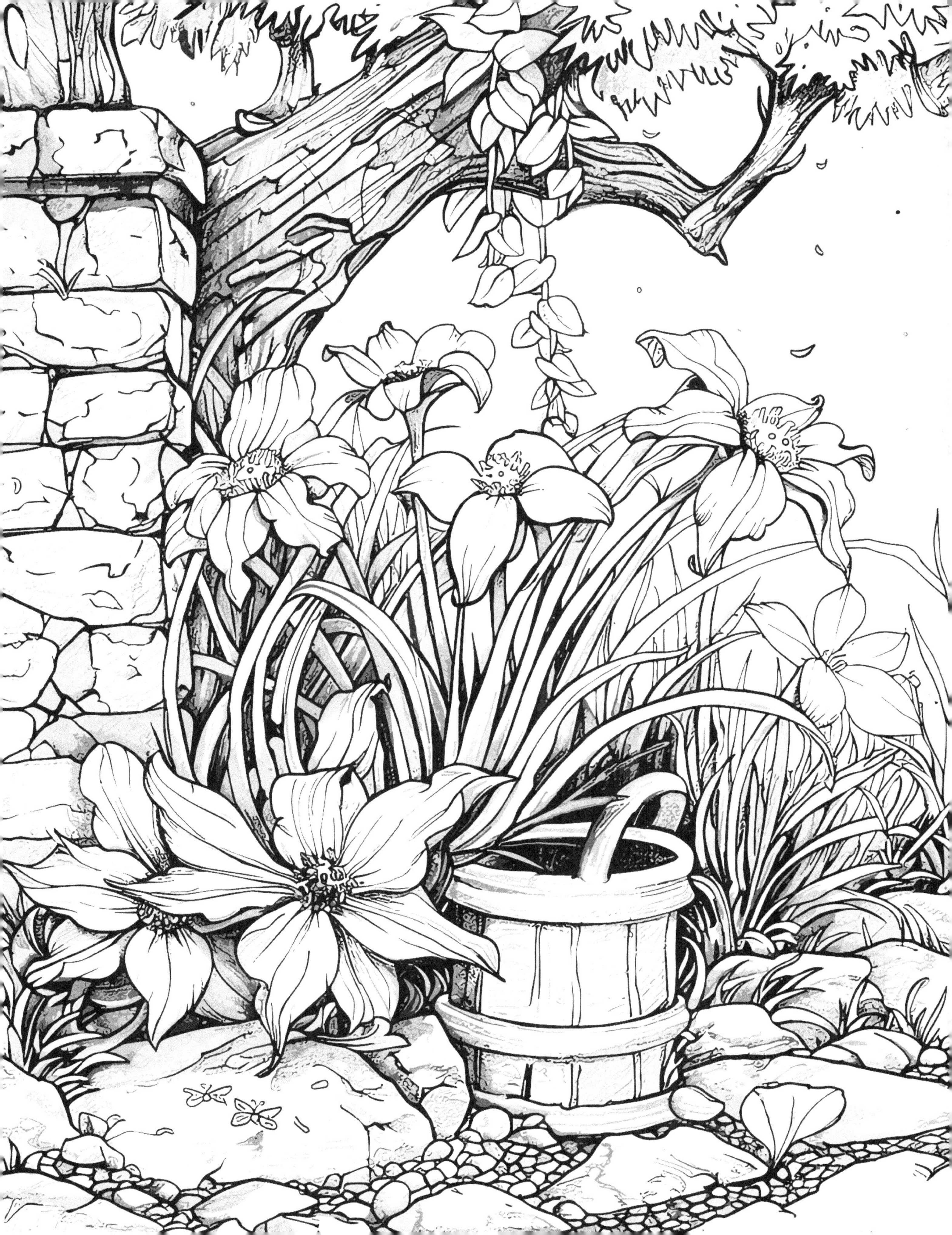

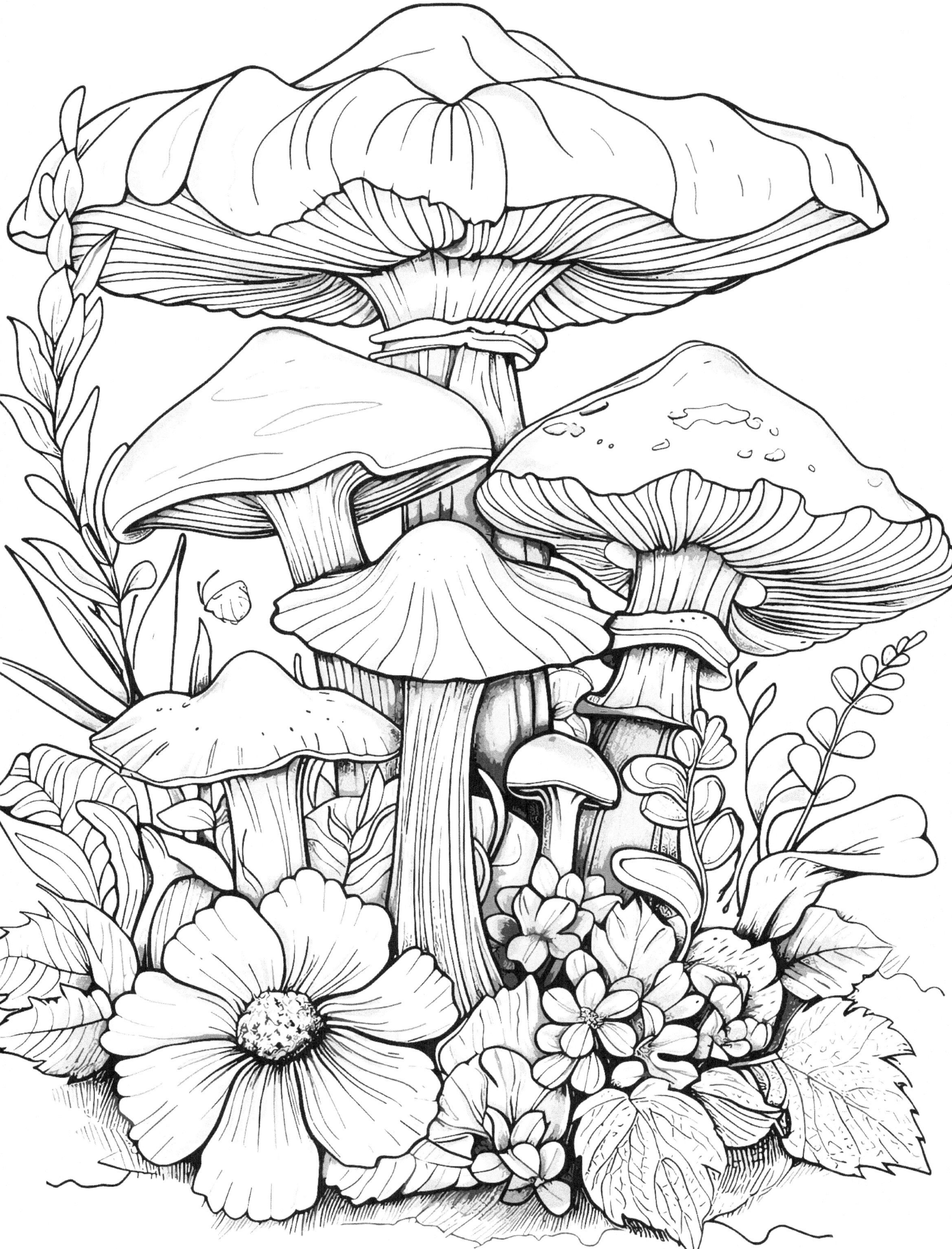

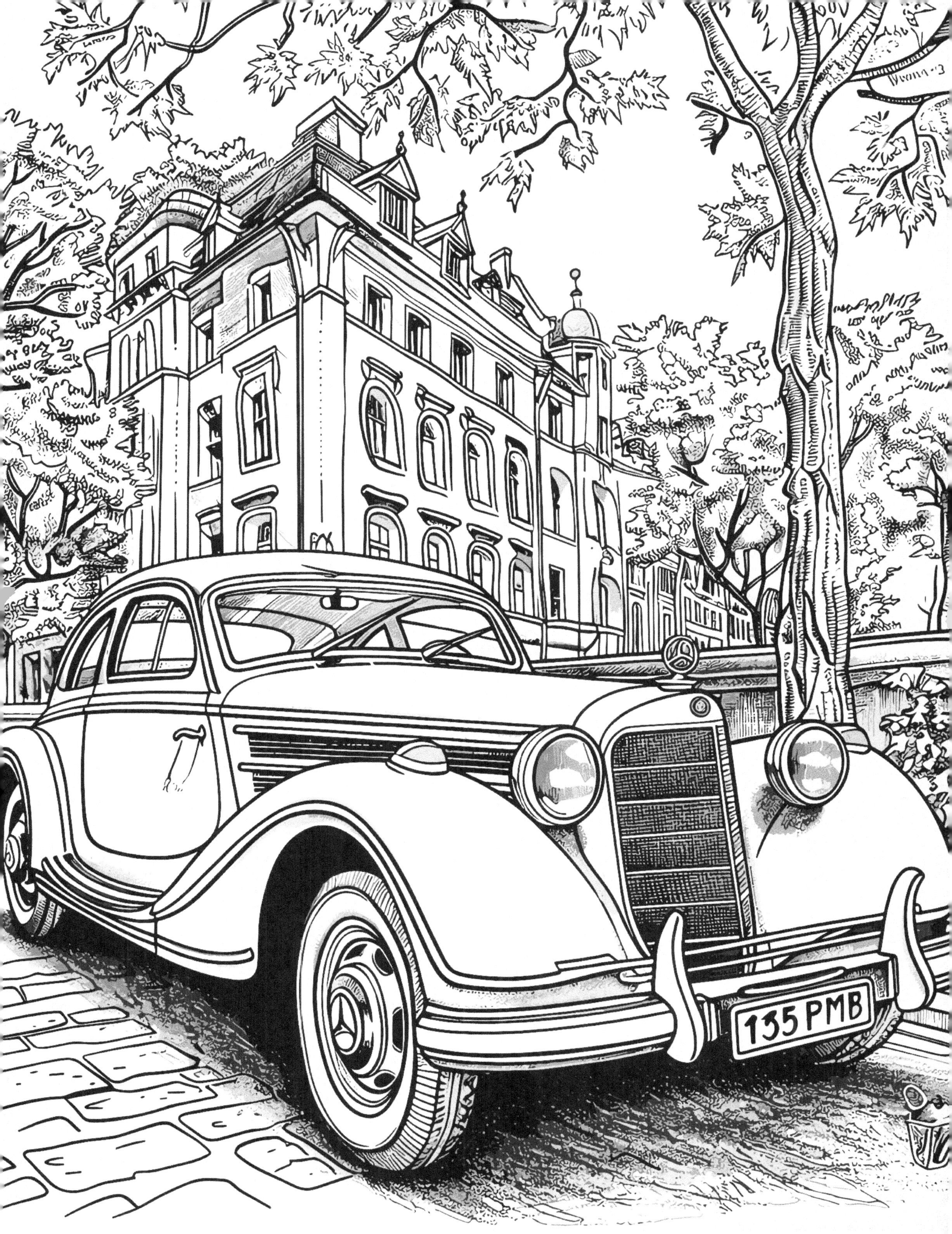
135 PMB

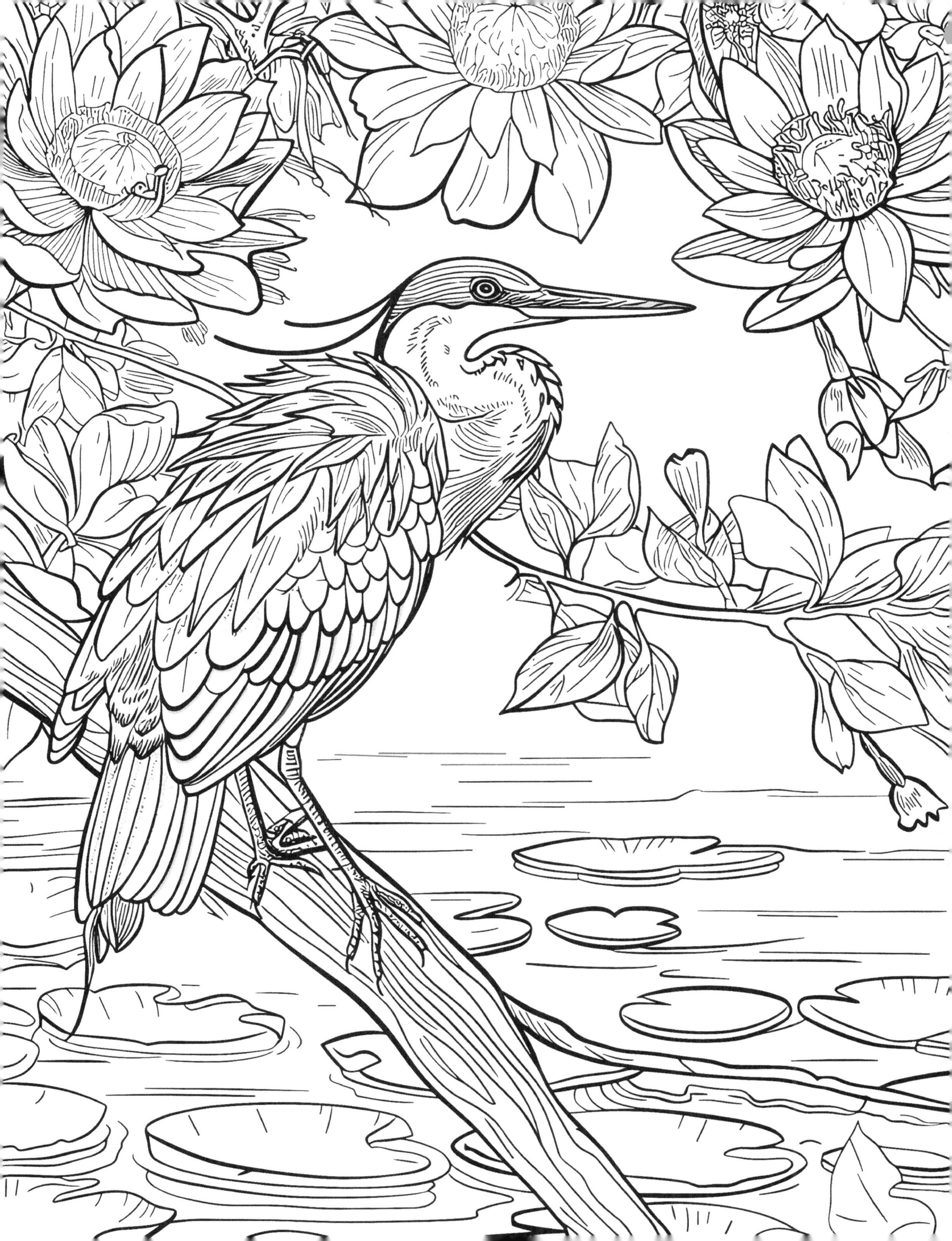

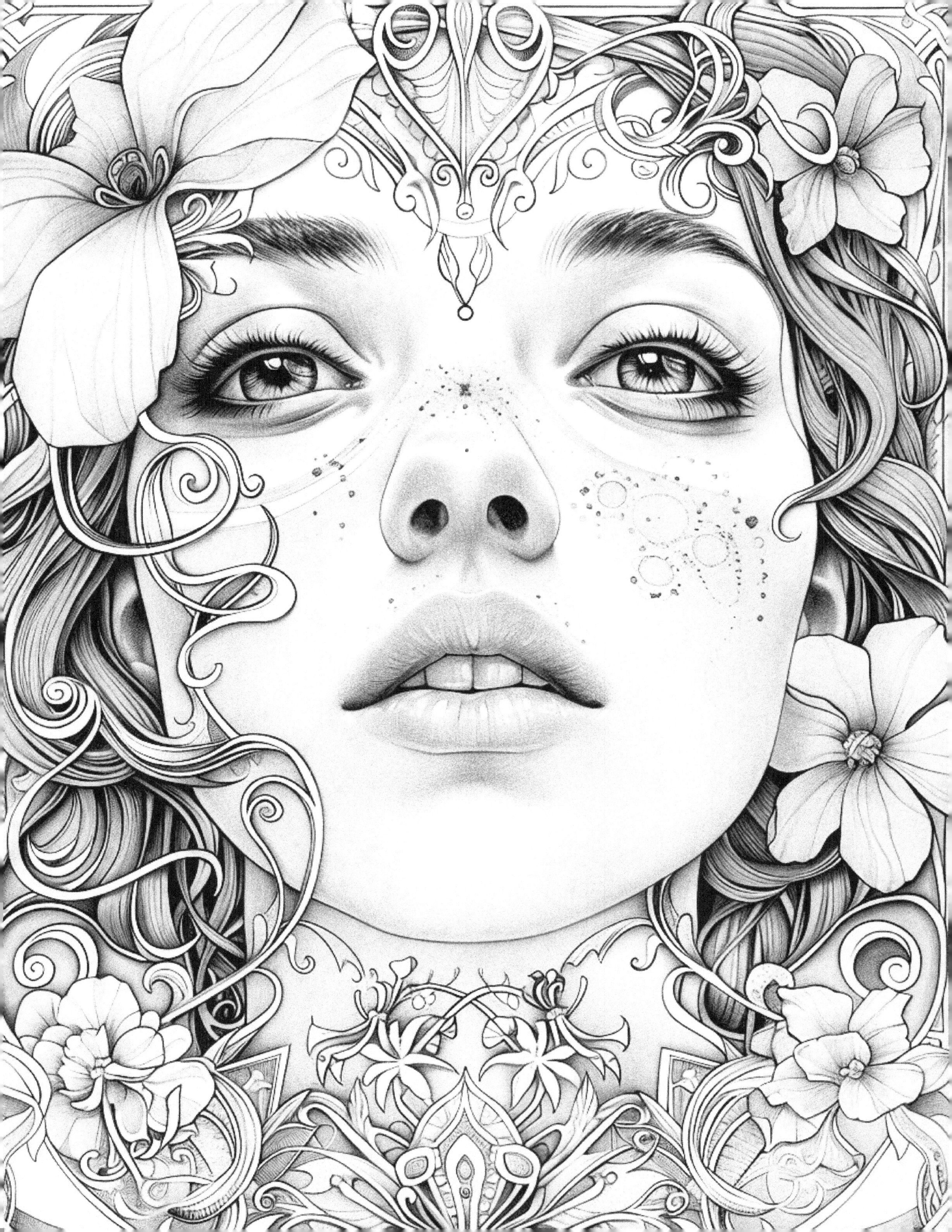

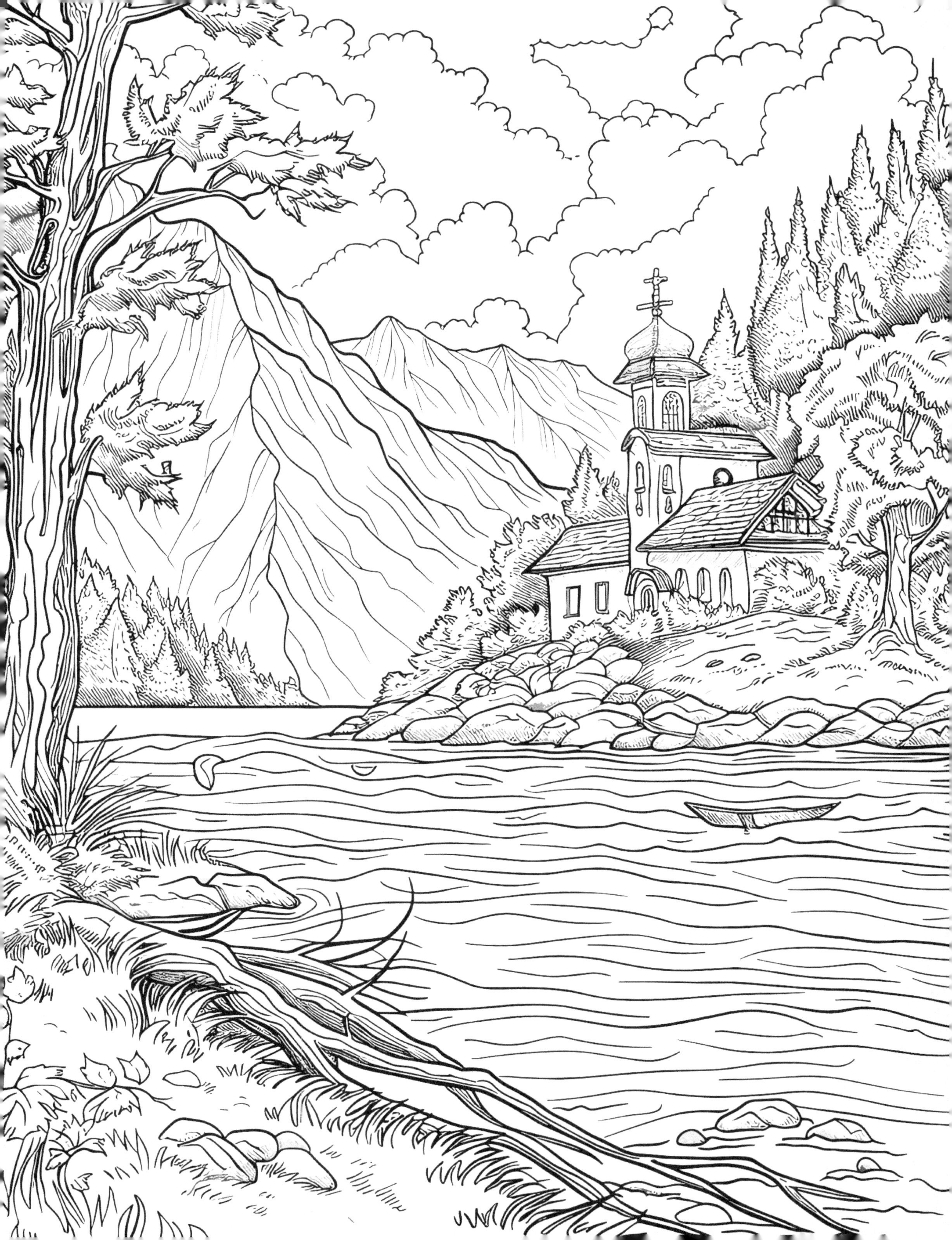

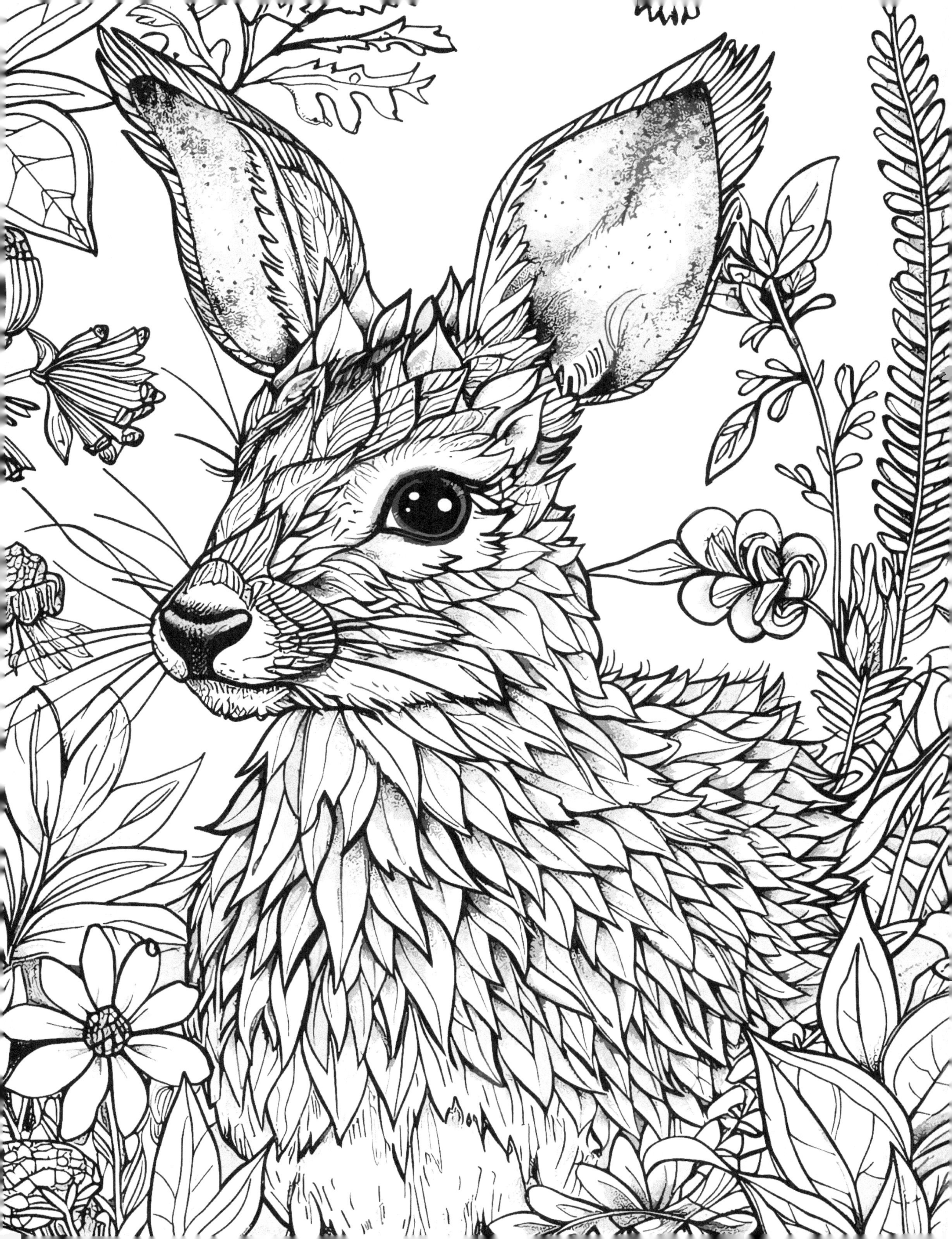

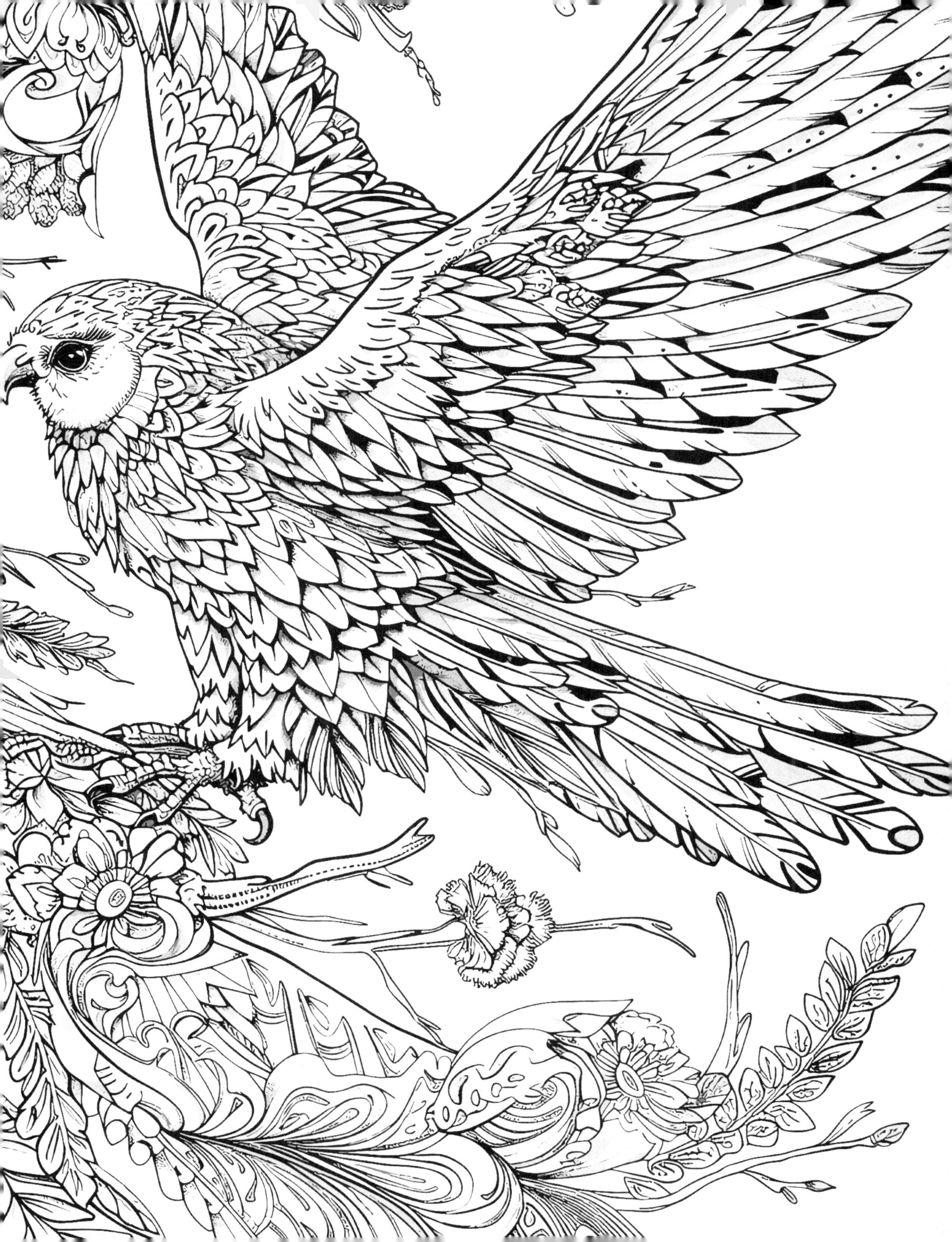

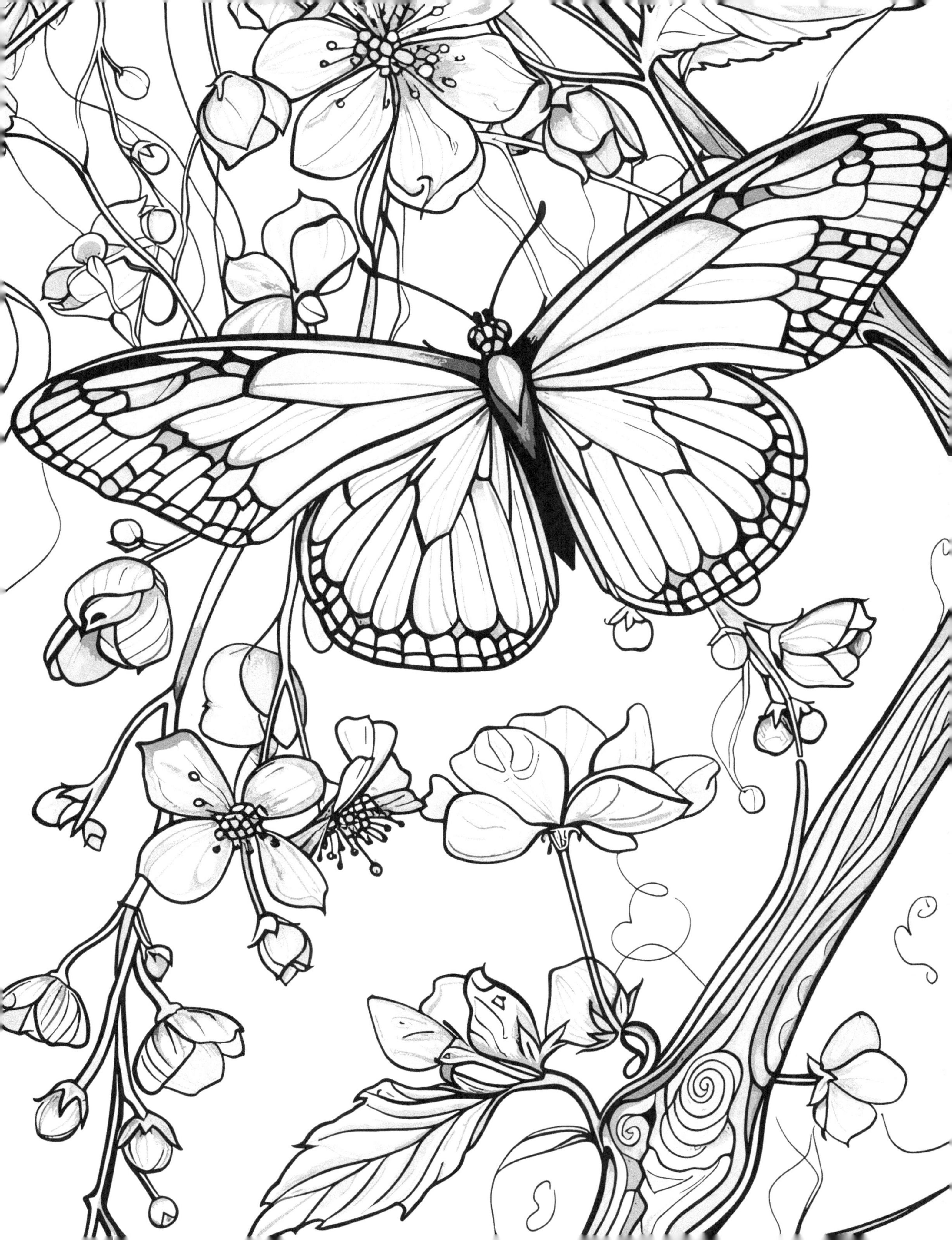

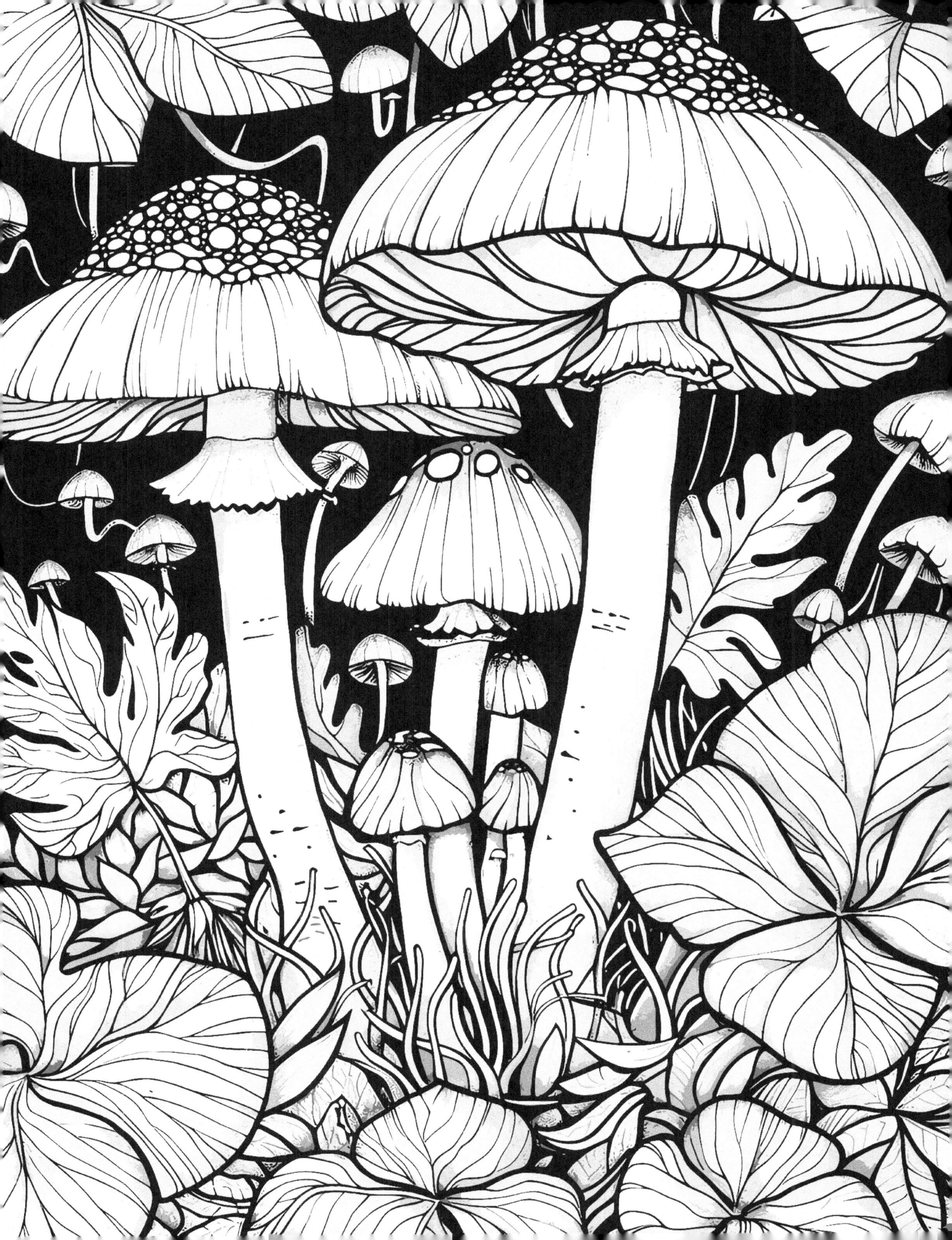

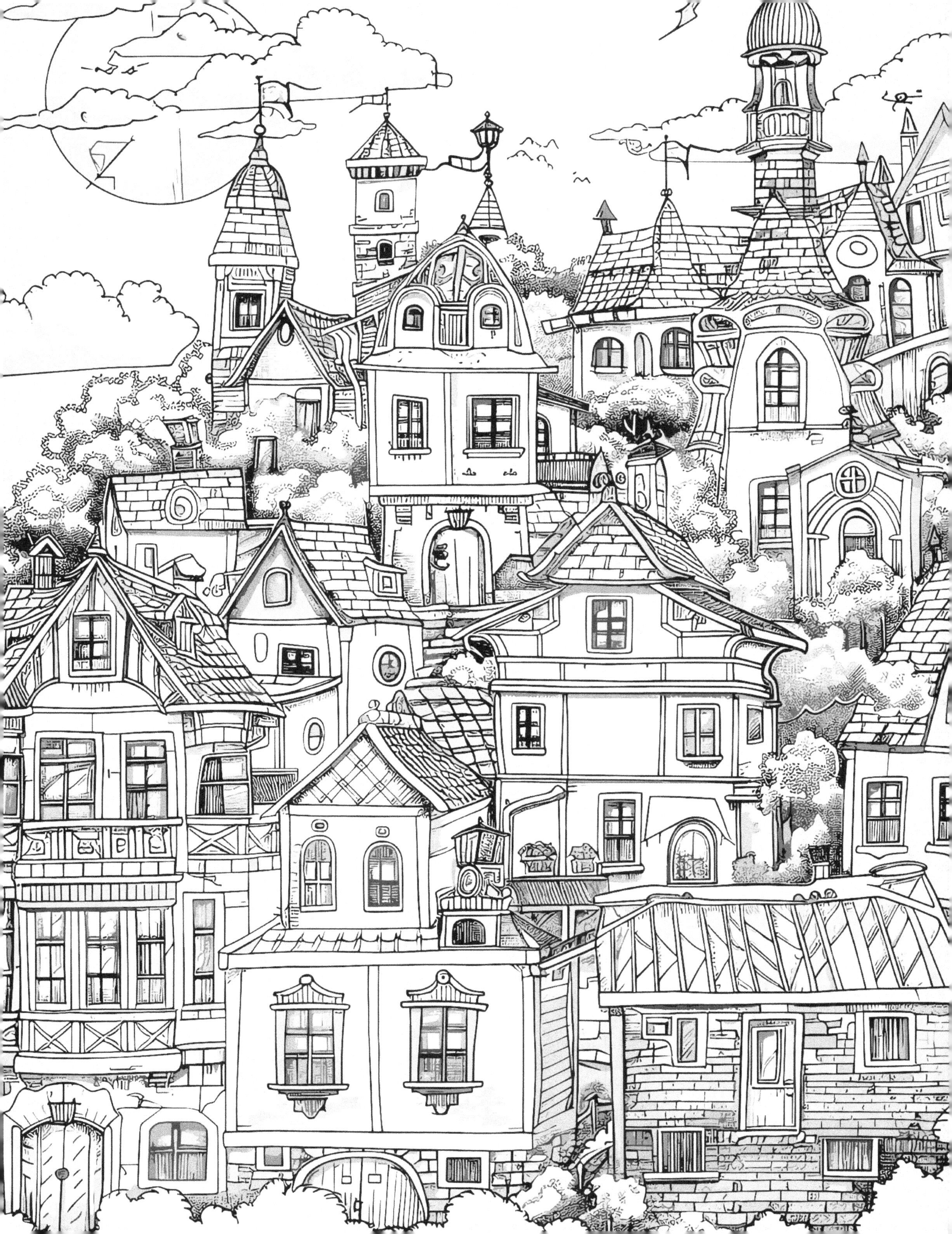

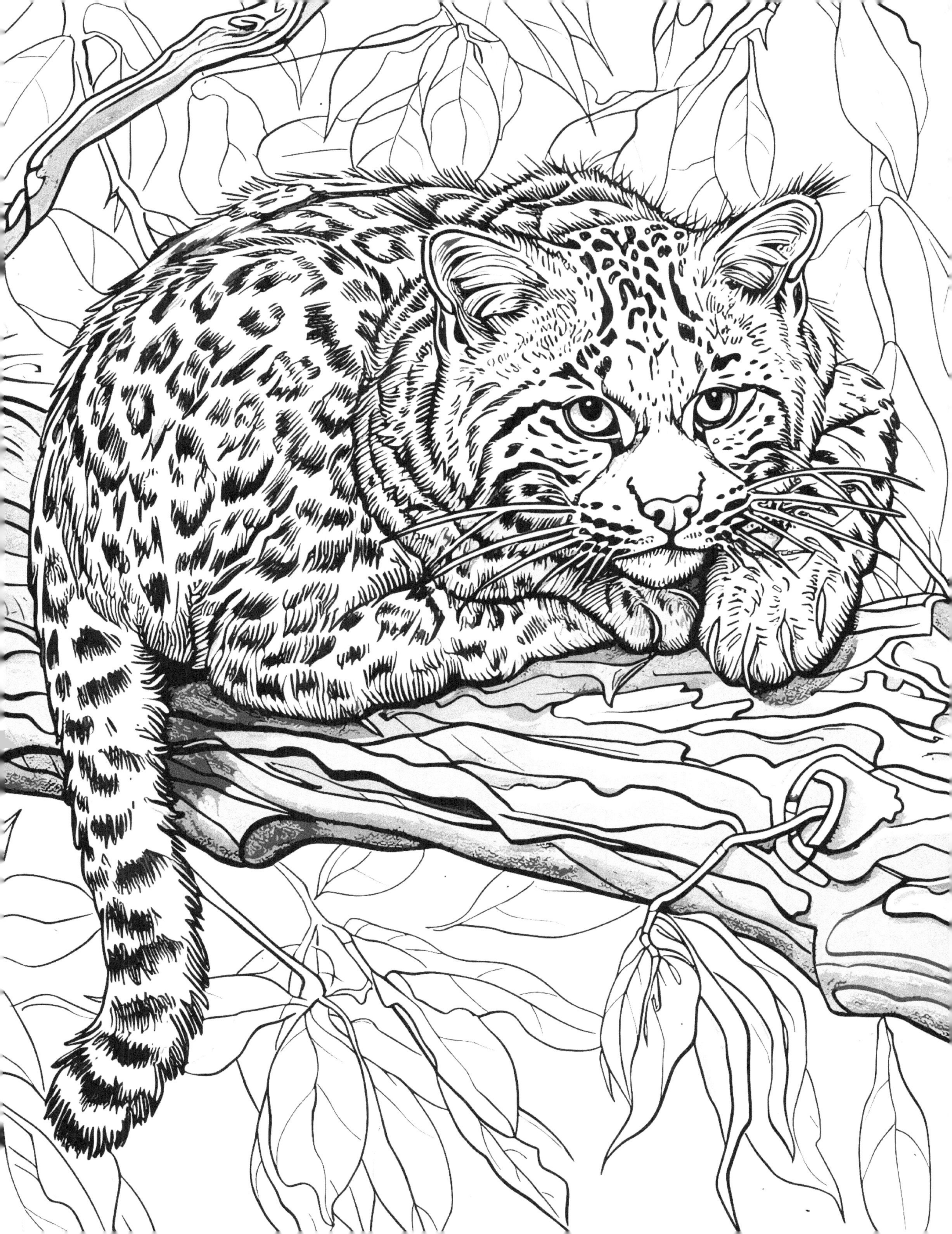

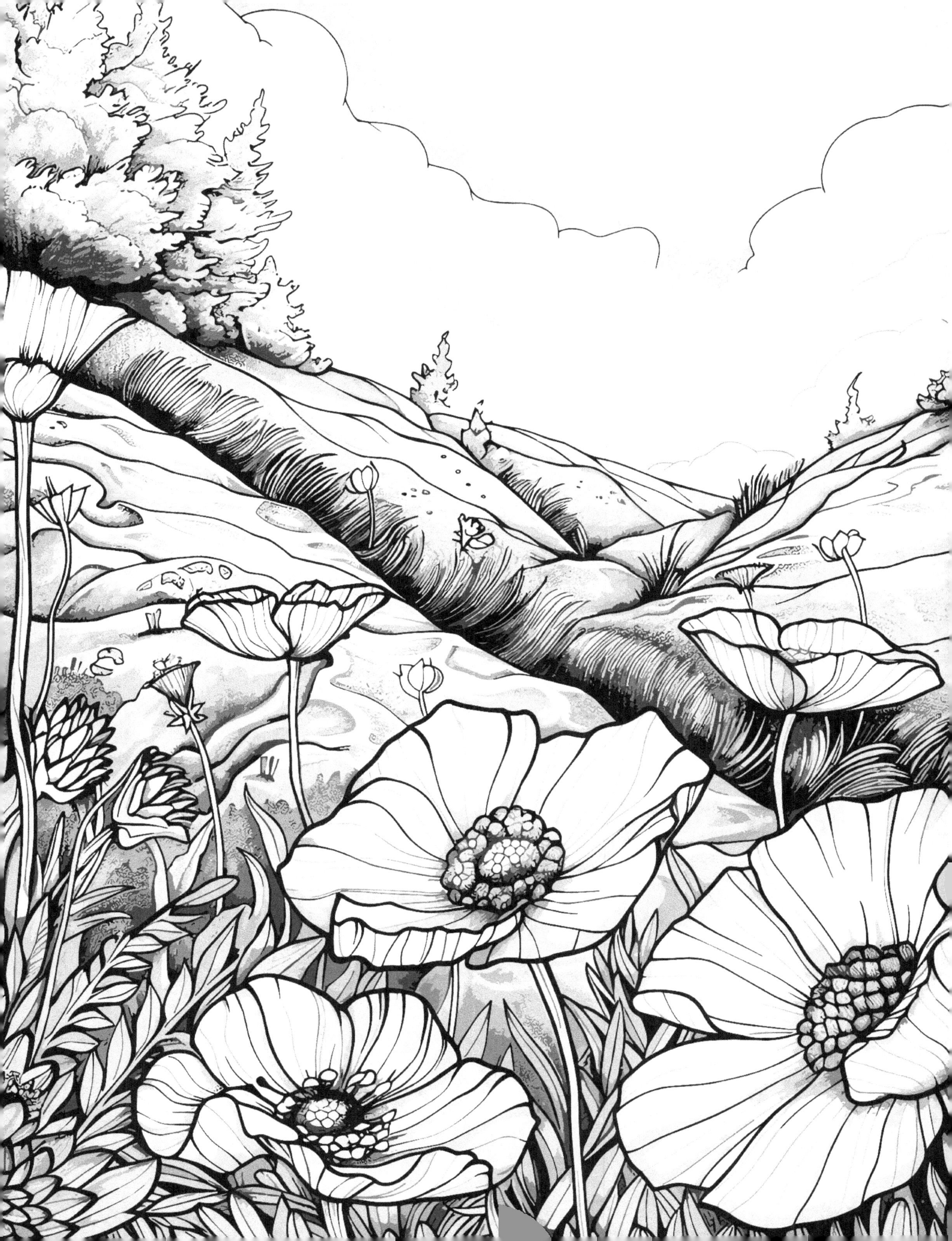

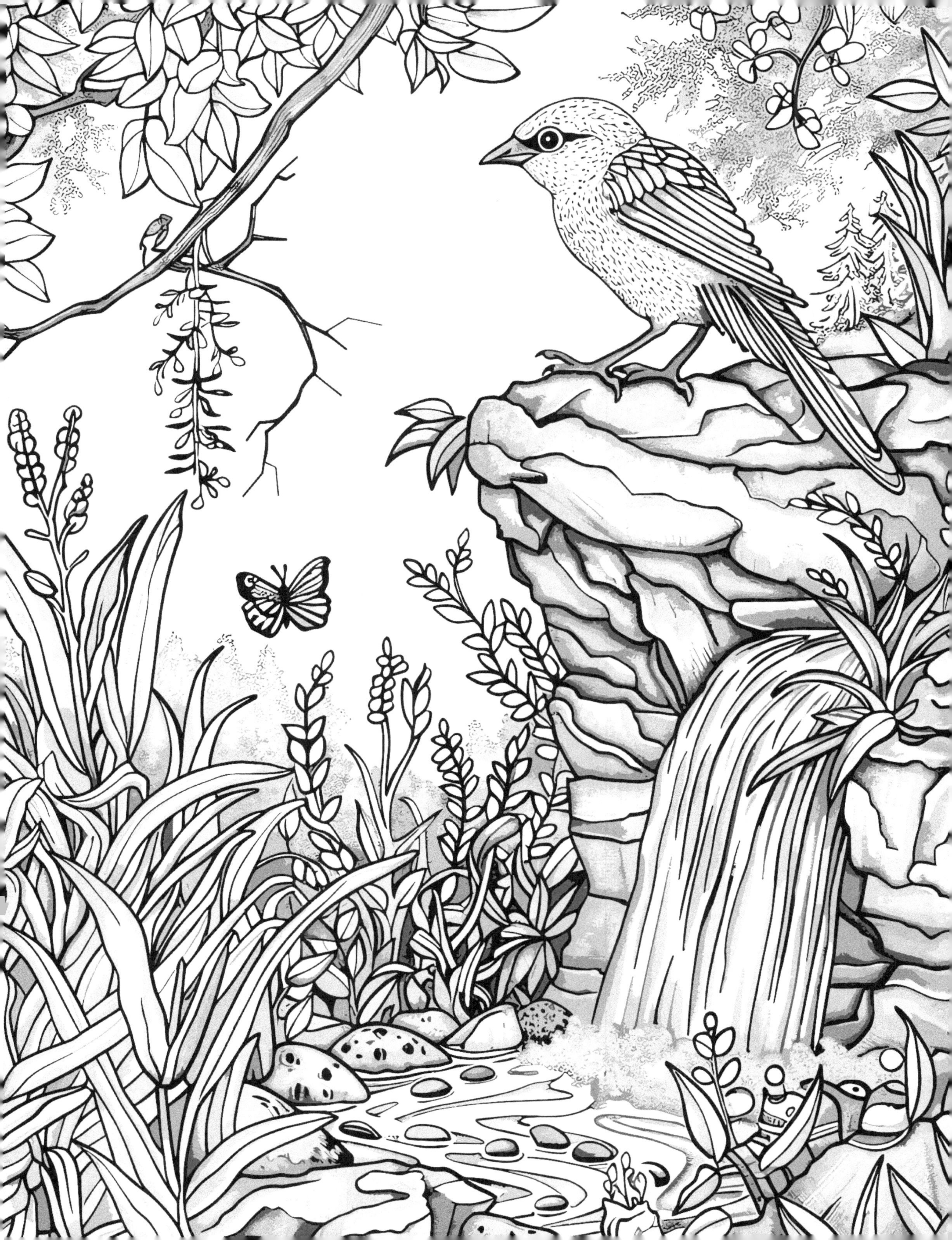

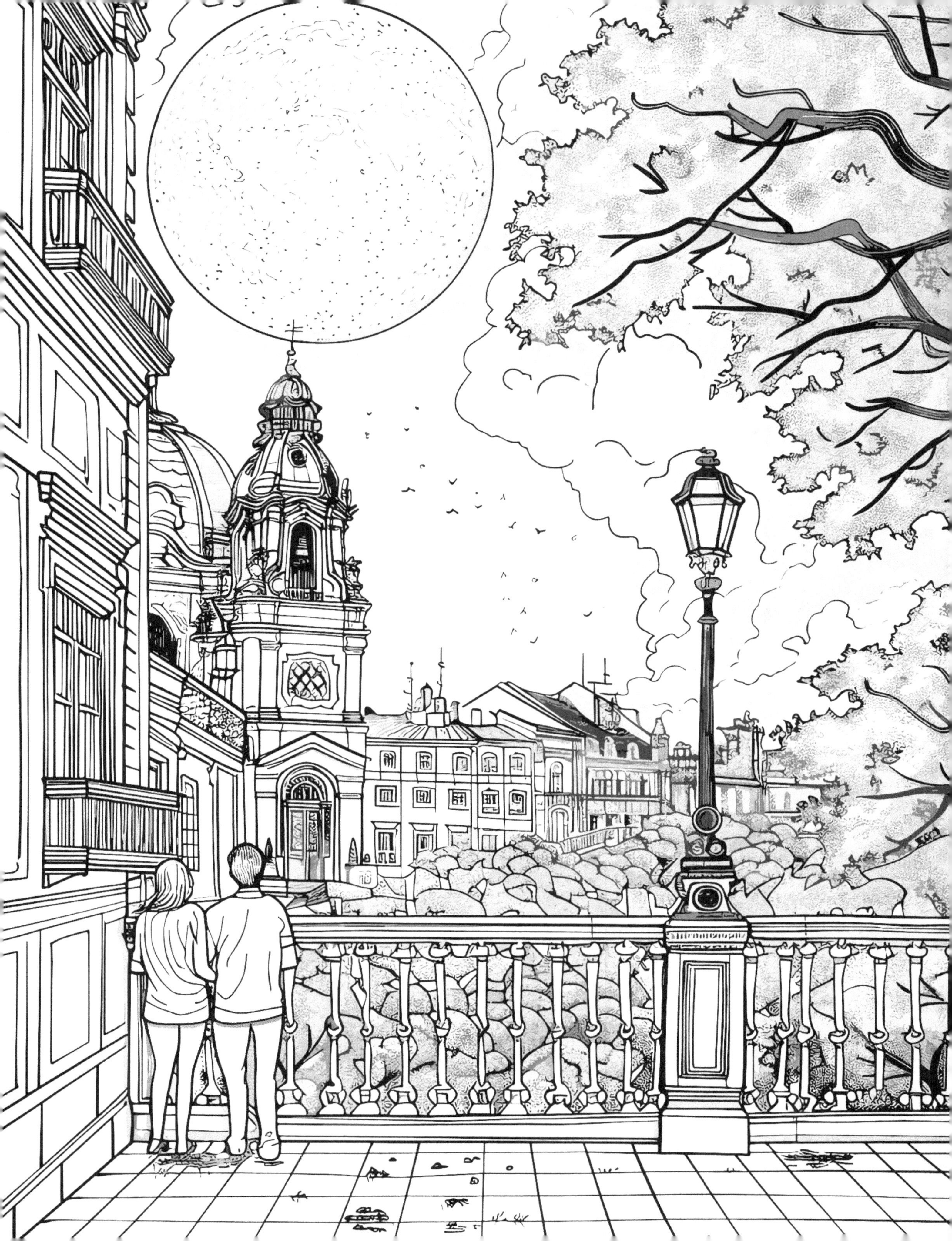

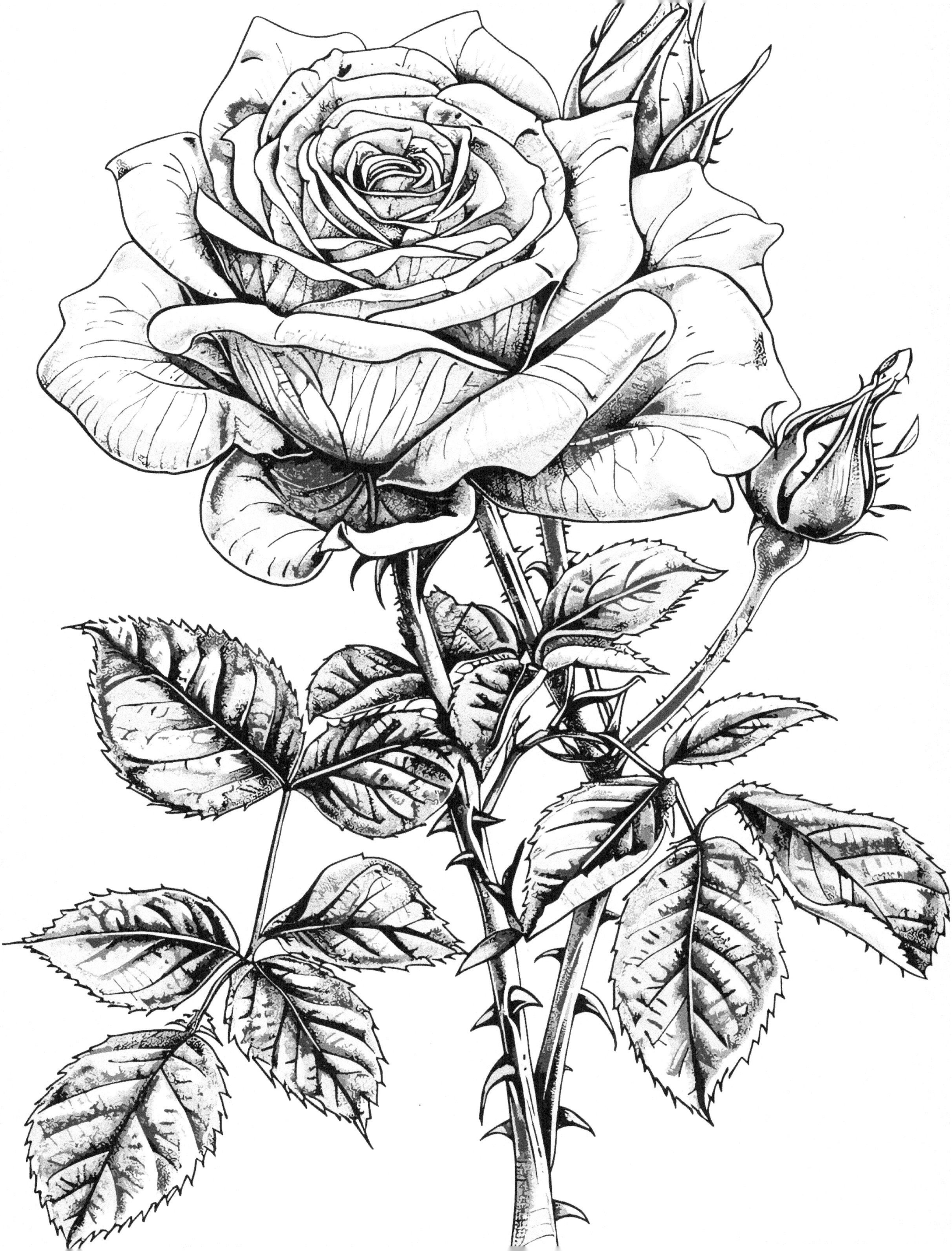

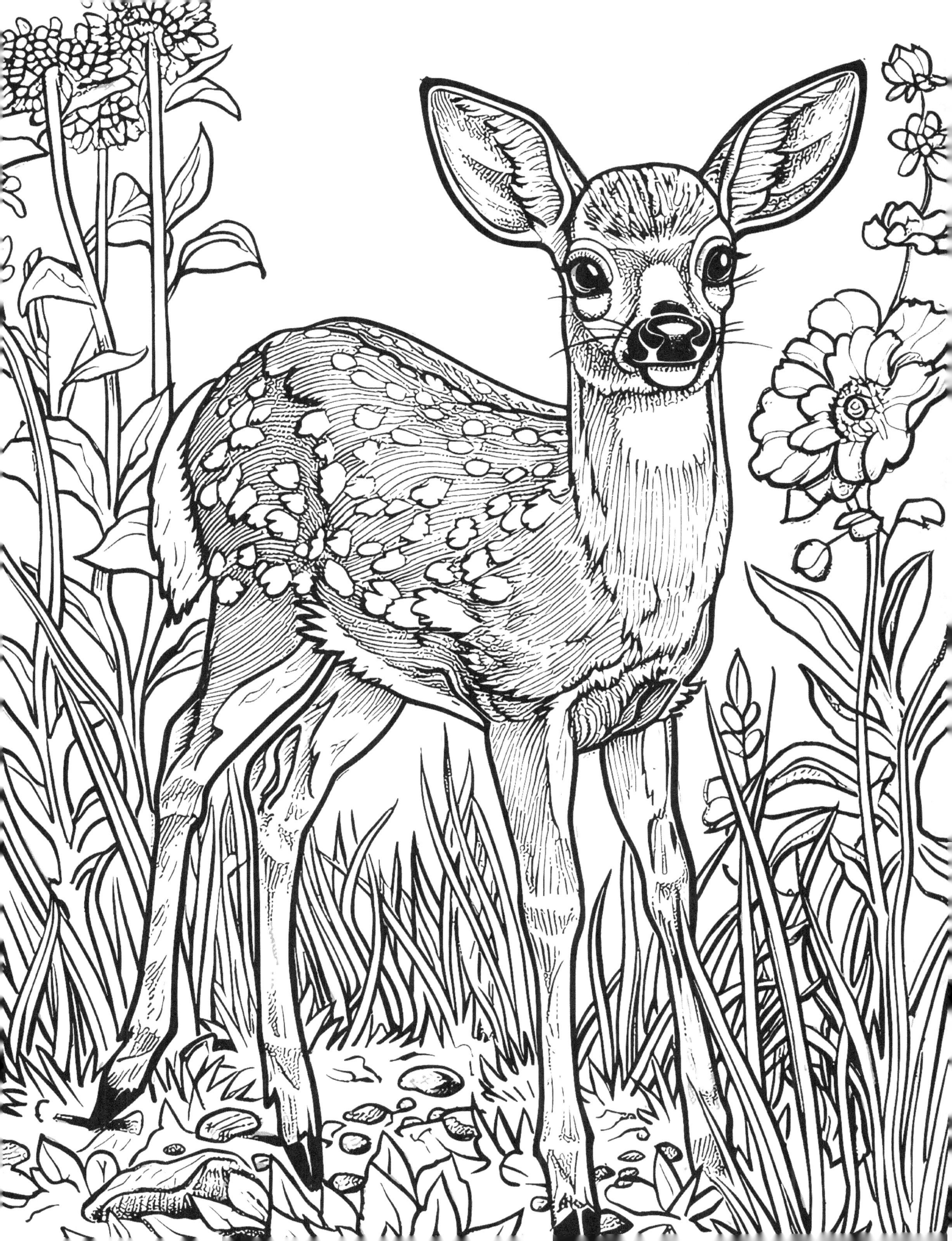

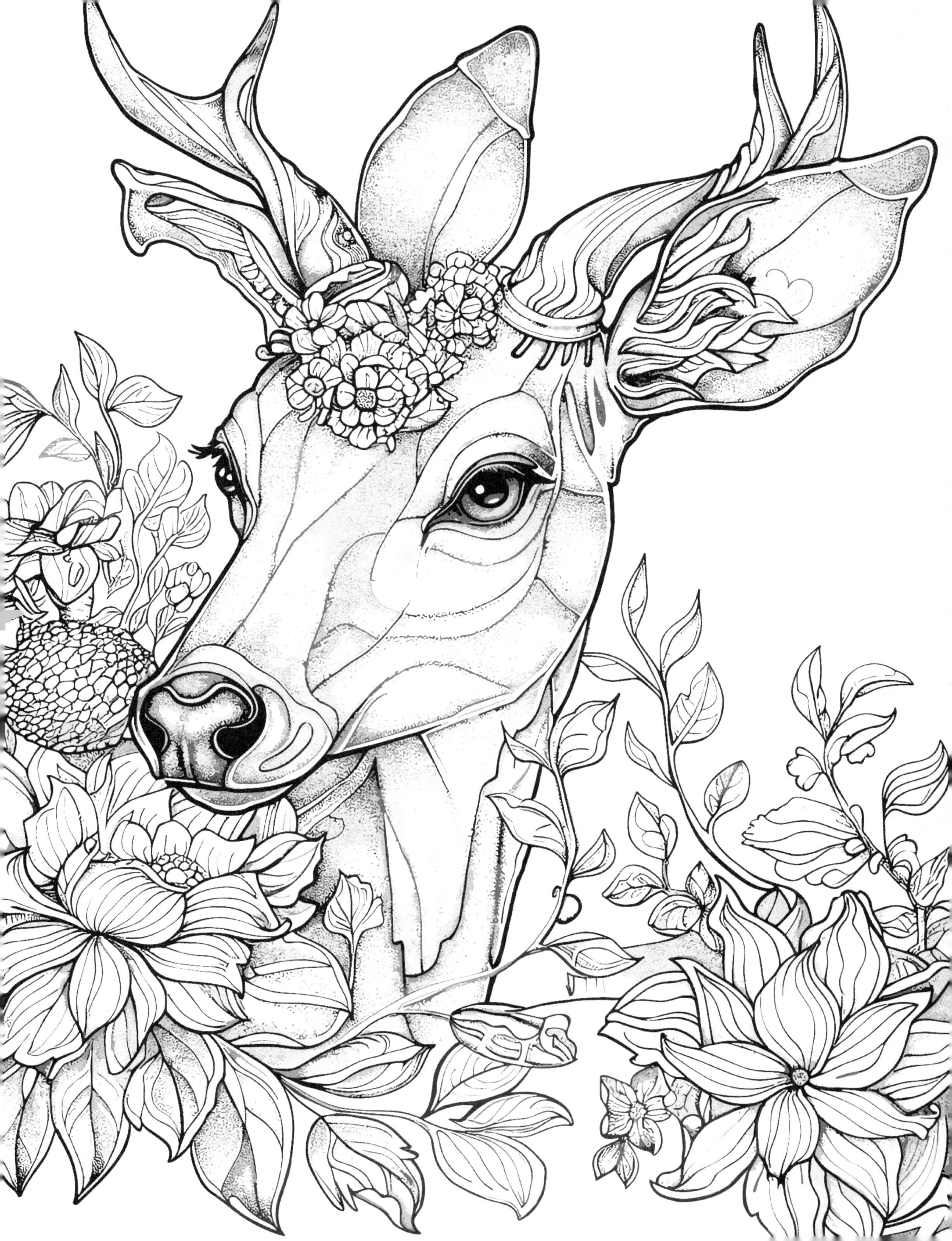

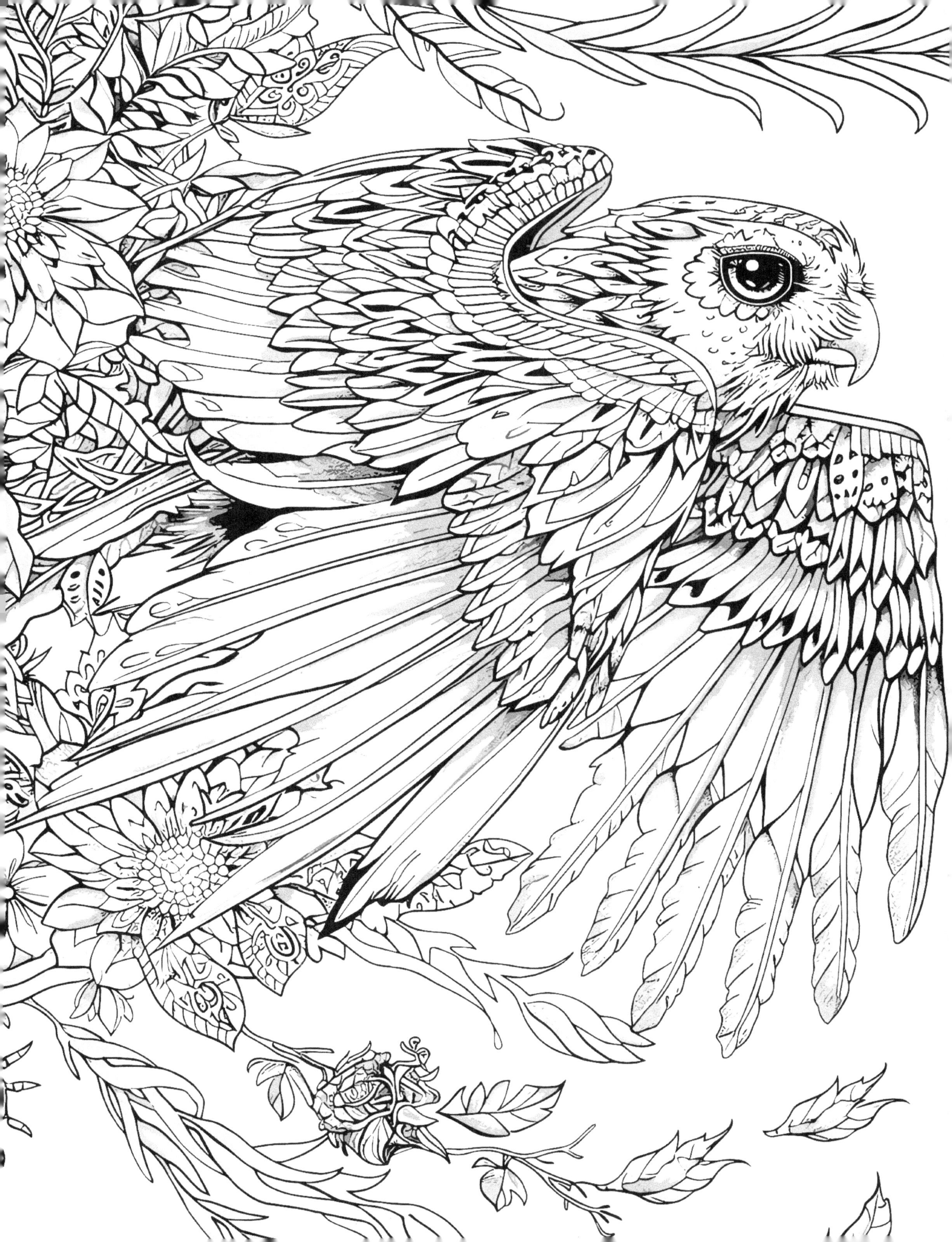

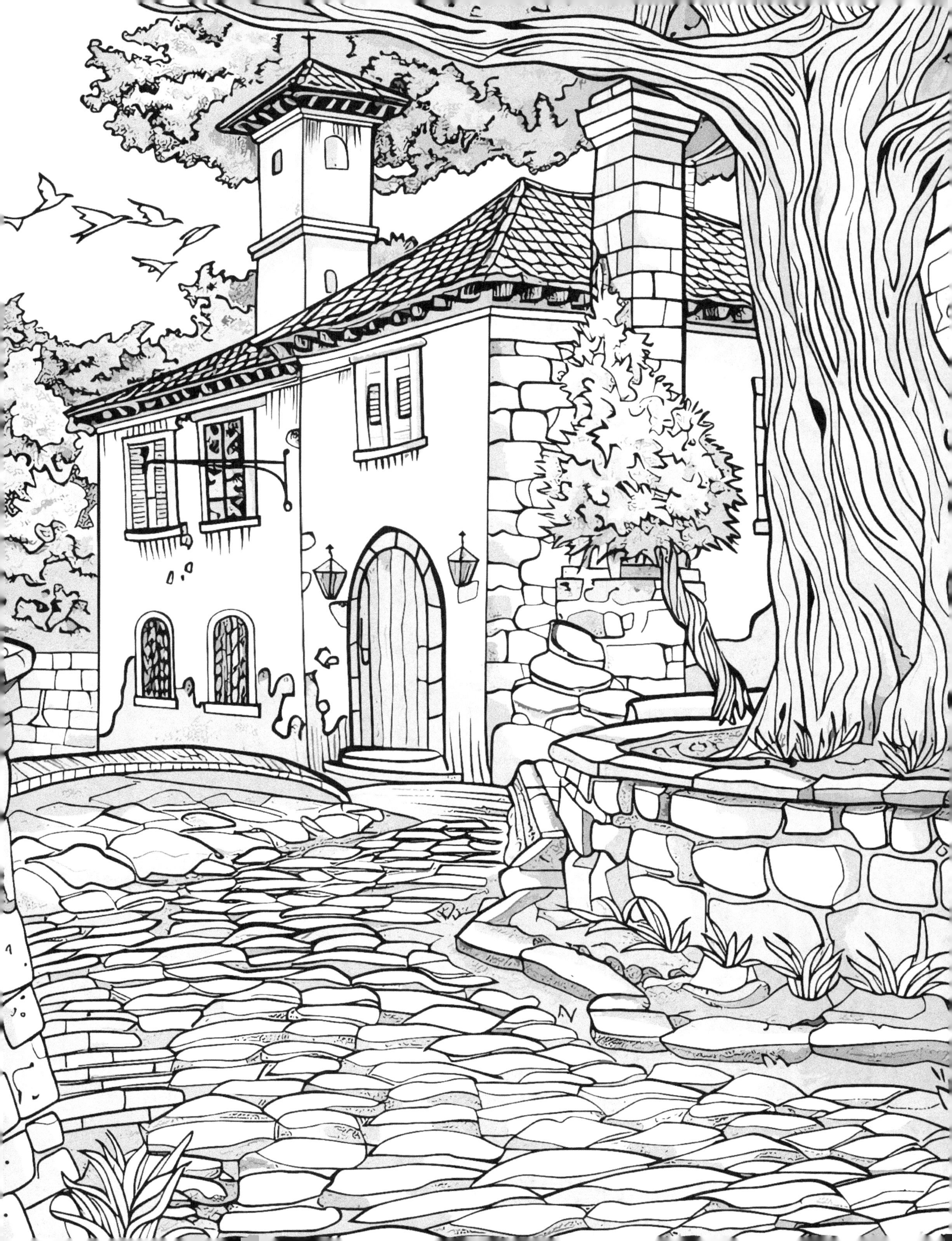

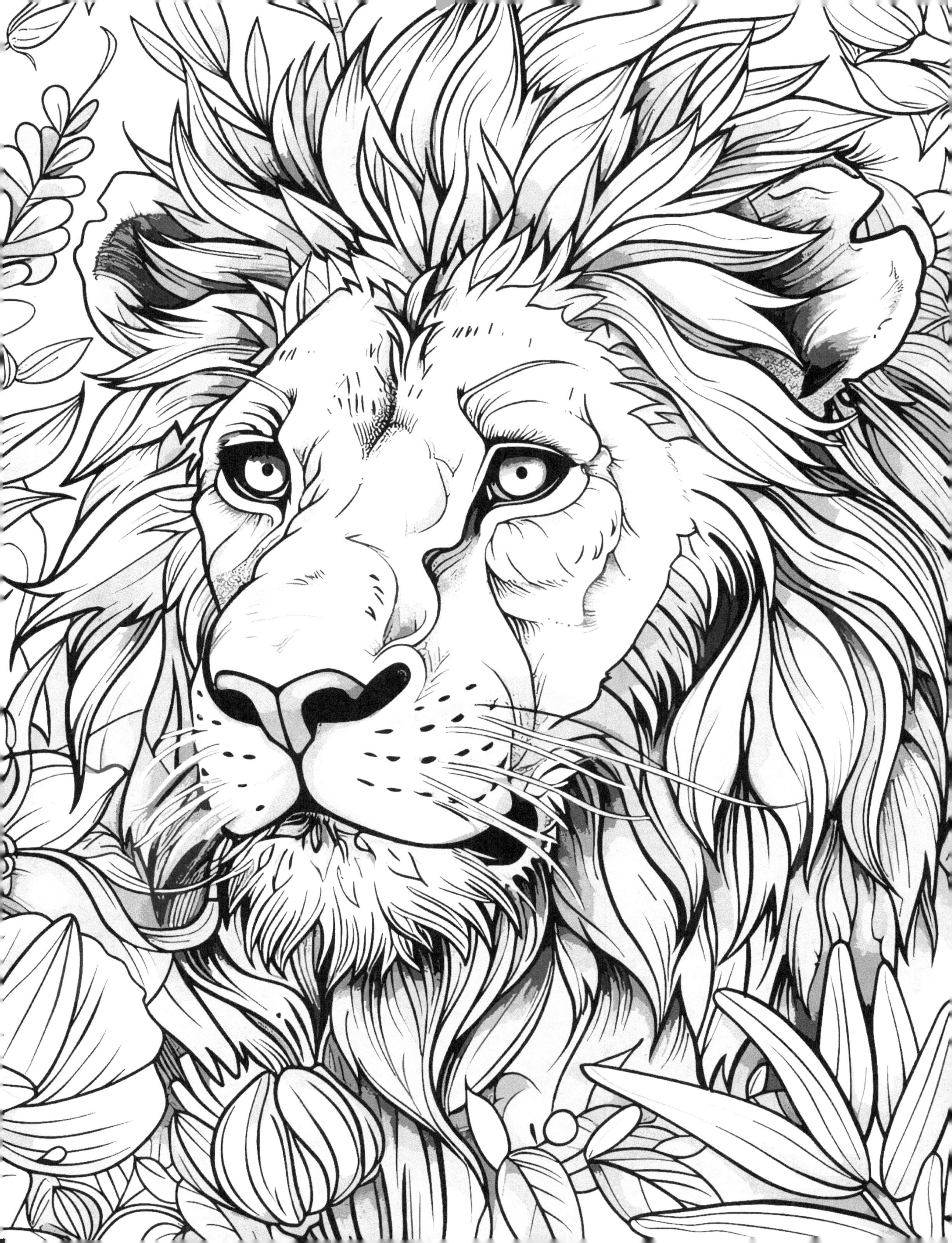

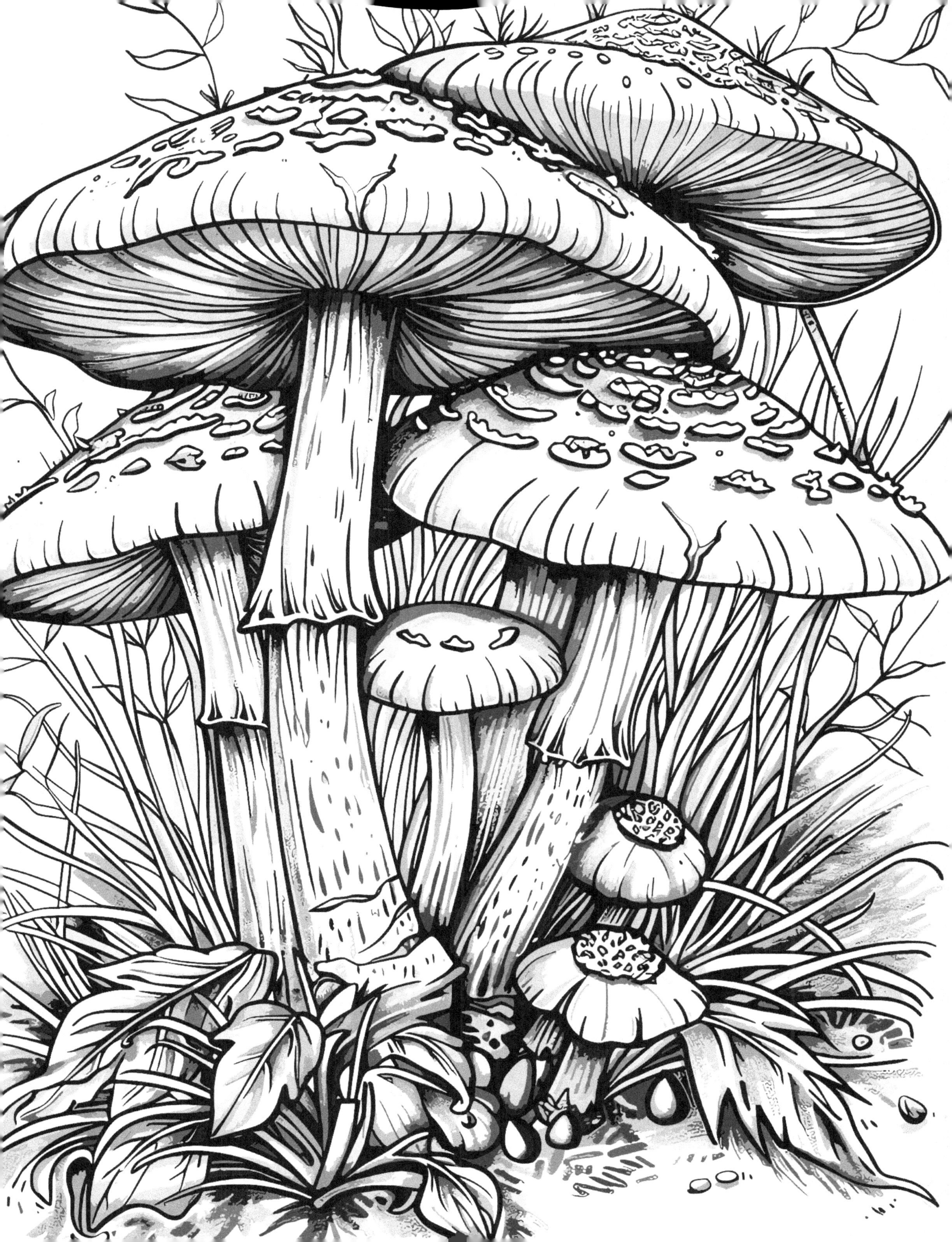

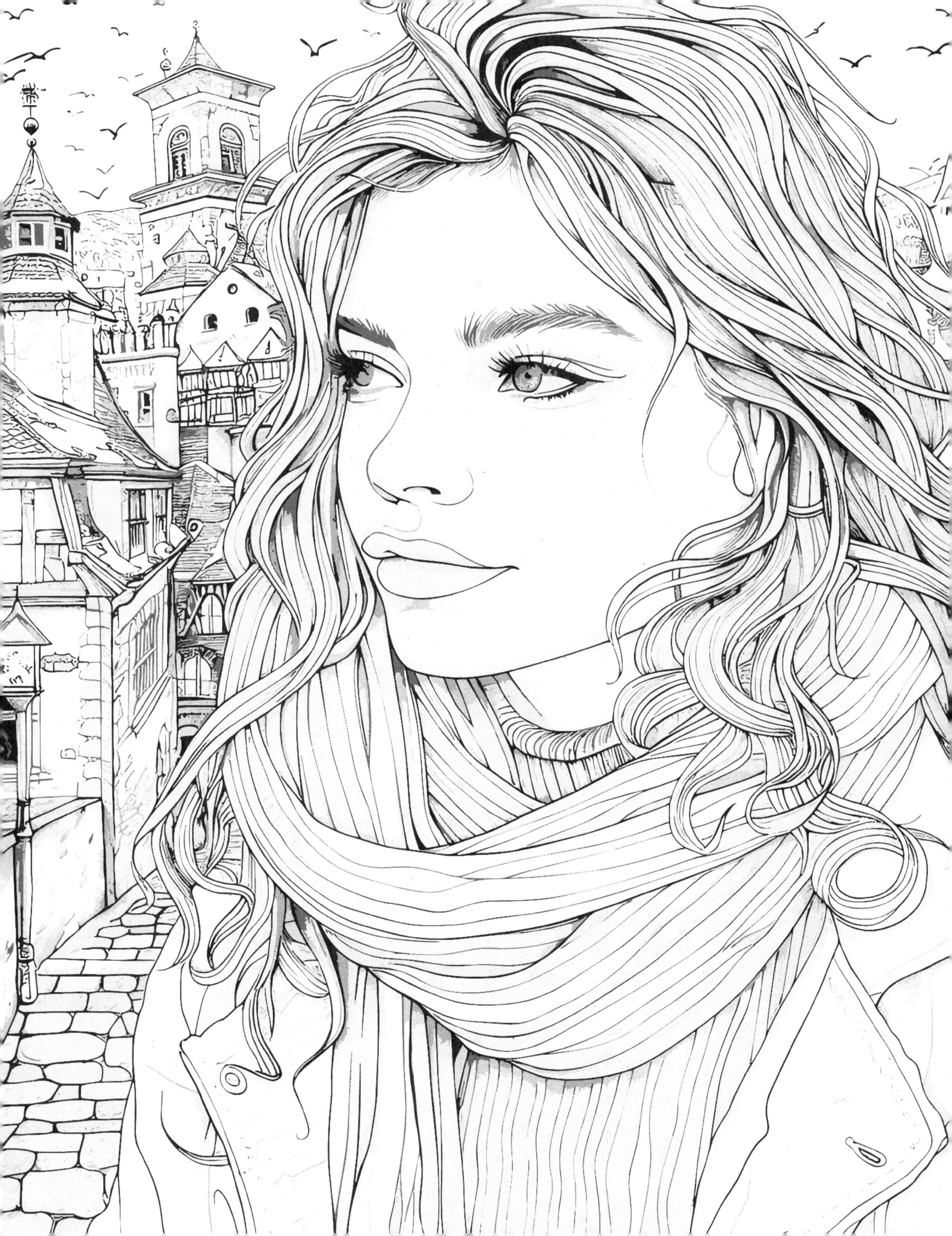

www.ingramcontent.com/pod-product-compliance
Lightning Source LLC
Chambersburg PA
CBHW082342220526
45470CB00008B/2603
9798326844675